Philosophy for the Masses: Metaphysics and More

David Bruce

Published by David Bruce, 2024.

Cover Photograph for *Philosophy for the Masses: Metaphysics and More*:

https://pixabay.com/photos/the-thinker-auguste-rodin-1881-1882-1144887/

Do you know a language other than English? If you do, I give you permission to translate this book, copyright your translation, publish or self-publish it, and keep all the royalties for yourself. (Do give me credit, of course, for the original book.)

PHILOSOPHY FOR THE MASSES: METAPHYSICS AND MORE

First edition. March 26, 2024.

Copyright © 2024 David Bruce.

ISBN: 979-8224651603

Written by David Bruce.

Table of Contents

Dedication

Dedicated to Carl Eugene Bruce and Josephine Saturday Bruce

My father, Carl Eugene Bruce, died on 24 October 2013. He used to work for Ohio Power, and at one time, his job was to shut off the electricity of people who had not paid their bills. He sometimes would find a home with an impoverished mother and some children. Instead of shutting off their electricity, he would tell the mother that she needed to pay her bill or soon her electricity would be shut off. He would write on a form that no one was home when he stopped by because if no one was home he did not have to shut off their electricity.

The best good deed that anyone ever did for my father occurred after a storm that knocked down many power lines. He and other linemen worked long hours and got wet and cold. Their feet were freezing because water got into their boots and soaked their socks. Fortunately, a kind woman gave my father and the other linemen dry socks to wear.

My mother, Josephine Saturday Bruce, died on 14 June 2003. She used to work at a store that sold clothing. One day, an impoverished mother with a baby clothed in rags walked into the store and started shoplifting in an interesting way: The mother took the rags off her baby and dressed the infant in new clothing. My mother knew that this mother could not afford to buy the clothing, but she helped the mother dress her baby and then she watched as the mother walked out of the store without paying.

***

The doing of good deeds is important. As a free person, you can choose to live your life as a good person or as a bad person. To be a good person, do good deeds. To be a bad person, do bad deeds. If you do good deeds, you will become good. If you do bad deeds, you will become bad. To become the person you want to be, act as if you already are that kind of person. Each of us chooses what kind of person we will become. To become a good person, do the things a good person does. To become a bad person, do the things a bad person does. The opportunity to take action to become the kind of person you want to be is yours.

Human beings have free will. According to the Babylonian Niddah 16b, whenever a baby is to be conceived, the Lailah (angel in charge of contraception) takes the drop of semen that will result in the conception and asks God, "Sovereign of the Universe, what is going to be the fate of this drop? Will it develop into a robust or into a weak person? An intelligent or a stupid person? A wealthy or a poor person?" The Lailah asks all these questions, but it does not ask, "Will it develop into a righteous or a wicked person?" The answer to that question lies in the decisions to be freely made by the human being that is the result of the conception.

A Buddhist monk visiting a class wrote this on the chalkboard: "EVERYONE WANTS TO SAVE THE WORLD, BUT NO ONE WANTS TO HELP MOM DO THE DISHES." The students laughed, but the monk then said, "Statistically, it's highly unlikely that any of you will ever have the opportunity to run into a burning orphanage and rescue an infant. But, in the smallest gesture of kindness — a warm smile, holding the door for the person behind you, shoveling the driveway of the elderly person next door — you have committed an act of immeasurable profundity, because to each of us, our life is our universe."

In her book titled *I Have Chosen to Stay and Fight*, comedian Margaret Cho writes, "I believe that we get complimentary snack-size portions of the afterlife, and we all receive them in a different way." For Ms. Cho, many of her snack-size portions of the afterlife come in hip hop music. Other people get different snack-size portions of the afterlife, and we all must be on the lookout for them when they come our way. And perhaps doing good deeds and experiencing good deeds are snack-size portions of the afterlife.

The Zen master Gisan was taking a bath. The water was too hot, so he asked a student to add some cold water to the bath. The student brought a bucket of cold water, added some cold water to the bath, and then threw the rest of the water on a rocky path. Gisan scolded the student: "Everything can be used. Why did you waste the rest of the water by pouring it on the path? There are some plants nearby which could have used the water. What right do you have to waste even a drop of water?" The student became enlightened and changed his name to Tekisui, which means "Drop of Water."

PREFACE

This book consists of a number of philosophical arguments that I find interesting and that I think that some other people may find interesting.

May you be struck by philosophical lightning.

My series of books on interesting philosophical arguments mainly consist of notes in essay form that I have made on the various books that I have used as textbooks in the philosophy courses that I have taught at Ohio University. These textbooks include various editions of the following:

- *Exploring Ethics*, by Donald M. Borchert and David Stewart
- *Exploring the Philosophy of Religion*, by David Stewart
- *Fundamentals of Philosophy*, by David Stewart and H. Gene Blocker
- *An Introduction to Modern Philosophy*, by Alburey Castell, Donald M. Borchert, and Arthur Zucker

I hope that other people find these notes in essay form useful.

METAPHYSICS
Chapter 1: Plato (427?-347 B.C.E.): The Phaedo

The *Phaedo* is the story of a man who is condemned to death.

In the *Phaedo* are described the final hours of life and the death of Socrates (469-399 B.C.E.), who was condemned to die by a jury in ancient Greece. The trial of Socrates was described in Plato's *Apology*.

Let me point out that Plato (427?-347 B.C.E.) was a student of Socrates, and that Socrates never wrote down his personal philosophy. In fact, there is some controversy over how much of what the character of Socrates says in Plato's dialogues is really what the historical Socrates believed. Most scholars believe that Plato expanded on the historical Socrates' ideas, so even though "Socrates" is the main speaker in most of Plato's dialogues, the ideas expressed by "Socrates" may be those of Plato.

However, the character of Socrates in Plato's "Apology," at least, may be very close to the historical Socrates, since the "Apology" is an early dialogue, and since Plato was present at the trial. However, Plato was not present at the historical Socrates' death.

At the end of the "Apology," Socrates has been condemned to die, but he tells his friends and the jury that death is nothing to be afraid of. According to Socrates, death is one of two things, neither of which we should fear.

The first possibility is that death is like a long, dreamless sleep, which Socrates describes as the most peaceful sleep you can have. In this case, death is the extinguishing of consciousness, and we will no longer be able to feel pain or fear.

The second possibility is that death is a journey to another place where one can meet and talk with the souls of the dead. This is also nothing to be afraid of. In this case, there is an afterlife in which we will retain our personal identities. Socrates would enjoy this, as he could talk philosophy with dead Greek heroes.

In the *Phaedo*, however, Socrates rejects the first possibility and argues for the second. In doing so, he engages in metaphysics, that branch of philosophy that tries to answer the question, "What is real?" Socrates argues that the soul is a real, immortal thing, and that when we die, our soul will survive the death of our body.

In the *Phaedo*, Socrates explains why he is not grieved at being condemned to die: "I should be wrong ... not to grieve at death, if I did not think I was going to live both with ... gods who are good and wise, and with men who have died and who are better than the men of this world. ... I am confident that the dead have some kind of existence, and, as has been said of old, an existence that is far better for the good than for the wicked."

In other words, Socrates is convinced that he is immortal. He goes on to explain that he believes that a human being is composed of two things: a body and a soul. Although our body will die and decay, our soul is immortal and incorruptible (in the sense that it cannot decay). Therefore, when our body dies, our soul — which is the best part of us — will live on. This idea, of course, makes Socrates a dualist, because he thinks that each member of Humankind is composed of two things.

Socrates also says that philosophers study "only dying and death." According to Socrates, philosophers despise the pleasures of the body, such as eating and drinking, instead choosing to pursue the pleasures of acquiring wisdom.

Why do philosophers despise the body and love the soul? Because the body is a hindrance in the acquisition of wisdom. The body gives us our five senses — seeing, hearing, smelling, touching, and tasting — but our senses deceive us. For example, a stick looks bent when part of it is placed in water.

In addition, according to Socrates, we are able to reason best when our body does not interfere. All of us know that it is difficult to study when we are hungry, or thirsty, or suffering from sunburn, or sleepy.

Socrates next makes a point that some things exist, although they are not visible. His friends agree with him that such things as absolute justice, absolute beauty, and absolute good exist although we cannot see them. In the life we lead now, we see a particular just person, a particular beautiful person, and a particular good person, but no one we see is absolutely just, beautiful, or good. However, according to Socrates, absolute justice, absolute beauty, and absolute good are real, and they are the objects of philosophic wisdom, although the body cannot sense them.

Therefore, for all these reasons, Socrates concludes that the body is a hindrance to the acquisition of wisdom. Socrates points out, "Verily we have learned that if we are to have any pure knowledge at all, we must be freed from the body; the soul by herself must behold things as they are."

This will occur only when the soul is freed from the body, as will occur at death.

Socrates then argues that our soul existed before we were born. This is one part of his argument that our soul is immortal. Later he will argue that our soul will continue to exist after we die.

To argue that our soul existed before we were born, Socrates talks about his theory of education. According to Socrates, "Learning is only a process of recollection." By that, he means that we don't acquire knowledge in this life; instead, we merely remember things we had learned when our soul was freed from our body. These are things that we forgot during the trauma of birth.

Socrates uses the concept of equality in his argument. We recognize the concept of equality. For example, I can show you two sticks and ask you if they are equal in length. You will reply either that they are or that they are not. In formulating your answer, you are using the concept of equality.

Of course, we are using our senses to perceive the two sticks, but that does not account for our knowledge of abstract equality. Abstract equality is different from the equality of two sticks that are equal in length. Seeing the two equal sticks make us recollect the concept of absolute equality, which the soul learned when it was freed of the body.

As Socrates concludes, "Then before we began to see, and to hear, and to use the other senses, we must have received the knowledge of the nature of abstract and real equality; otherwise we could not have compared equal sensible objects with abstract equality...."

Just as we learned the knowledge of absolute equality before our soul was united with our body, Socrates states, so too we learned the knowledge of absolute good, absolute beauty, absolute justice, and absolute holiness.

Socrates sums up his argument in this way: " ... if it be the case that we lost at birth the knowledge which we received before we were born, and then afterward, by using our senses on the objects of sense, recovered the knowledge which we had previously possessed, then what we call learning is the recovering of knowledge which is already ours." In other words, learning is recollecting.

Socrates has argued that our soul existed before we were born — that is the time when we learned about such things as absolute equality. Next, he argues that our soul will continue to exist after we die. In doing this, he in part speaks about things that are compound and composite (composed of many parts) things and things that are not compound and composite (that is, things that are composed of only one part).

Our body is compound and composite and is made up of many elements. When we die, our body will decay. Its various elements will disperse and go their separate ways. Our body will become a part of the soil in which we are buried and the elements that made up our body may become a part of a living plant.

However, Socrates believes that the soul is not compound and composite — that is, that it is not made up of many parts. Because of that, it will not decay after we die. According to Socrates, there are two kinds of existence: the visible and the invisible. The visible kind of existence is always changing. For example, your body changes constantly. At one time you were an infant whose diapers frequently needed changing; now you are an adult.

Our body is an example of the visible kind of existence, but our soul is an example of the invisible kind of existence. The invisible kind of existence never changes. For example, absolute equality never changes. And since our soul is a part of this kind of existence, it can never change and so it can never cease to exist.

In conclusion, Socrates asks his friend Cebes, "... is it not the nature of the body to be dissolved quickly, and of the soul to be wholly or very nearly indissoluble?" Cebes, of course, agrees.

Note: The quotations by Plato that appear in this essay are from his dialogue *Phaedo*, translated by F. J. Church.

Chapter 2: Epicurus (341-279 B.C.E.): First Principles of Materialism

Epicurus (341-279 B.C.E.) was an ancient Greek philosopher who was a Materialist. As such, he believed that reality consists of matter and space. The matter that exists, according to Epicurus, is composed of atoms.

The first Greeks who were Materialists and Atomists were Leucippus and Democritus. Epicurus was one of their followers.

In his "Letter to Herodotus," Epicurus wrote about his beliefs concerning the universe. He also wrote about his theory of sense perception and gave some advice about achieving tranquility in life.

According to Epicurus, the universe has always existed and it consists of "material bodies and void." The bodies are made up of atoms, which are "indivisible and unchangeable." The universe is boundless, and in it is an infinite number of atoms. Therefore, the number of bodies and the void (space) of the universe are endless.

Epicurus concludes that the atoms, which combine to make up the things that we see, "exist in so many different shapes that the mind cannot grasp their number," because otherwise we could not account for the great variety of objects which the atoms make up. The possible shapes of the atoms are an incomprehensible, but not quite infinite, number, while the number of atoms of each shape is infinite.

According to Epicurus, "The atoms move without interruption through all time. Some of them fall in a straight line; some swerve from their courses; and others move back and forth as the result of collisions." The swerving causes some atoms to hit other atoms, and because of the different shapes of the atoms, some atoms become connected to other atoms. Atoms combining together make up the things that we see.

Furthermore, Epicurus believes that there is an infinite number of worlds. The Earth is one world, but there are many more worlds in the universe. Some worlds are like the Earth; other worlds are unlike the Earth.

Epicurus also gives his theory of sense perception. He writes, "... there are images of the same shape as the solid bodies from which they come but in thinness far surpassing anything that the senses can perceive." These images emanate from the things we see. The images are called by Epicurus "idols." The idols strike the eye, and because of this, we are able to see the object from which the idols emanate.

According to Epicurus, these images or idols "are of a texture unsurpassed in fineness. For this reason, their velocity is also unsurpassed ...." In addition, the emanating of the idols is continuous, and therefore their creation is constantly occurring.

Epicurus next provides an account of the possibility of error. Certainly, we are occasionally mistaken, but what accounts for this? According to Epicurus, "Whatever is false and erroneous is due to what opinion adds (to an image that is waiting) to be confirmed, or at least not contradicted, by further evidence of the senses, and which then fails to be so confirmed (or is contradicted)."

We fall into the possibility of error when we go beyond what we perceive. It is possible for me to see someone, think that I have seen a friend of mine, go up to the person and say hi, and then discover that I was mistaken and that the person I saw is actually a stranger. All I actually perceived was a human being, but I went beyond what I perceived and mistakenly thought that I had perceived a friend.

Epicurus also makes a distinction between primary and secondary qualities. Primary qualities are those qualities that belong to the objects themselves (size, shape, weight, motion), while secondary qualities are those qualities that are produced in our mind by those objects (colors, tastes, sounds).

According to Epicurus, the atoms have what we call primary qualities. In Epicurus' words, "We must suppose that the atoms possess none of the qualities of visible things, except shape, mass, and size, and whatever is a necessary concomitant of shape."

Epicurus believes that human beings have a soul; however, he does not believe that human beings have an incorporeal soul. The soul, like the body, is composed of atoms, and when we die, the atoms of the soul disperse. That means that Epicurus believes that our soul is corporeal and that we are mortal. When we die, our body and our soul both disintegrate, and that is the end of us.

However, being mortal is actually a good thing, according to Epicurus. Too many people fear death because they are afraid of what happens after death. They are afraid of being punished by the gods for their sins. However, if

Epicurus is right, this is not something that we need to fear. Death results in the extinguishing of consciousness, and we will be neither rewarded nor punished after death.

Epicurus next gives his theory about how we gave names to objects. According to Epicurus, human nature does things first because circumstances suggest that some actions be done, and second because human reason thinks about these actions and comes up with better ways of doing them. Thus, we may start gathering food because we are hungry, then later we may start growing food because reason suggests that this will give us a more stable food supply.

Names arise in the same way. Objects arouse certain feelings and impressions in us, and we express those feelings and impressions by naming those objects. Epicurus writes that people emitted "air from their lips formed in harmony with each of the experiences and impressions." People did this individually at first, but then reason suggested a better way: Within each nation people agree on a special name for a certain object. This allows people to better communicate with each other.

In addition, Epicurus believes that we ought not to fear the gods. The motions of the heavenly bodies are not due to the gods; they are due to the forces that act on the atoms.

Epicurus believes that the gods exist. (The ancient Greeks were polytheistic.) However, he also believed that the gods don't concern themselves about us at all. Once again, however, Epicurus thought that this was a good thing. If something bad happens, such as a plague, we need not worry that the gods sent the plague to punish us for our sins. The gods are aloof and neither reward us for our good deeds nor punish us for our bad deeds.

Even today, some people think that AIDS was sent by God to punish bad people (even though innocent infants acquire AIDS). Epicurus would deny that God sends plagues to punish people.

Epicurus' philosophy was concerned with the acquisition of tranquility. He lived in interesting times (an ancient Chinese curse is, "May you live in interesting times") when Alexander the Great's generals were busy carving up the empire after Alexander died. This resulted in many refugees, including Epicurus and his family, fleeing scenes of warfare.

This led Epicurus in his philosophy to stress ways of reducing anxiety and of achieving tranquility. Thus his emphasis on not being afraid of death and not being afraid of the gods.

Interested readers should be aware that Epicurus provides more information for leading a tranquil life in his "Letter to Menoeceus."

Note: The quotations by Epicurus that appear in this essay are from his "Letter to Herodotus," translated by Russel M. Geer.

Chapter 3: George Berkeley (1685-1753): Idealism

George Berkeley (1685-1753) was a believer in Idealism, which denies the reality of physical matter. According to Idealism, reality is mental, not physical. In his *Three Dialogues Between Hylas and Philonous*, Berkeley argues against Materialism and for Idealism. Hylas defends the Materialist position and Philonous defends the Idealist position. In other words, Philonous defends Berkeley's position.

Basically, Berkeley will argue that the only things we directly experience are ideas (redness, solidity, wetness, hotness, etc.). Since we do not directly experience any kind of underlying material substance, we cannot conclude that material substance exists. As you can tell, Berkeley is an empiricist — he believes that knowledge comes from the five senses.

In the *Three Dialogues*, Philonous' (that is, Berkeley's) main thesis is expressed: "... there is no such thing as *material substance* in the world." This appears to go against common sense, as Hylas says, but Philonous is prepared to mount a defense of his thesis.

Before doing so, however, Philonous argues that his Idealism does not deny the principles and theorems of the sciences. Since these principles and theorems are "universal intellectual notions, and consequently independent of matter," Idealism does not deny them.

For example, according to *The Concise Columbia Encyclopedia*, "If during a time t a body travels over a distance s, then the *average speed* of the body is s/t." There is no mention of matter here; the mathematical formula mentions "a body," but both Materialism and Idealism can account for the existence of bodies. A Materialist will say that a body such as a red ball is a material object possessing the quality of redness, while an Idealist will say that a body such as a red ball is a bundle of ideas (that is, sensible qualities) that includes the quality of redness.

Philonous does what many good philosophers do at the beginning of their philosophical investigations: He defines an important term he will be using. Defining a term at the outset of a philosophical investigation can avoid misunderstandings later.

In this case, the term to be defined is "sensible things." "Sensible" here means perceived by the senses — seeing, hearing, tasting, touching, and smelling. The definition that Philonous and Hylas agree to is *"sensible things are those only which are immediately perceived by sense."* The things that we perceive by seeing include light, colors, and figures (shapes); by hearing, sounds; by tasting, tastes; by smelling, odors; and by touching, tangible qualities.

However, one thing that we *cannot* perceive by the senses is the cause of the things we sense. Thus, if I hear a sound, I perceive the sound by the use of the sense of hearing, but I cannot perceive the cause of the sound. For example, if I am on the street and hear a piano playing (but don't see a CD player or a person playing a piano), I don't know if someone is playing a CD tape of piano music or if I am overhearing someone playing the piano in their apartment.

Of course, I can use *reason* to deduce the cause of the sound I hear, but reason is different from immediately perceiving something by the use of the senses. In the case of the piano music, even if I see someone seated at the piano and moving his arms, I may be mistaken about the cause of the piano music if I use my reason to deduce that the person I see is playing the piano. It could a player piano and the person may be pretending to play the piano. (This happens in a scene from the 1971 movie *Harold and Maude*, starring Ruth Gordon and Bud Cort.)

To understand Berkeley's ideas, you need to know what secondary and primary qualities are. Secondary qualities are those qualities (colors, tastes, sounds) that are produced in our mind by objects, while primary qualities are those qualities (size, shape, weight, motion) that are supposed to belong to the objects themselves.

Philonous is now ready to begin arguing that the qualities we perceive are qualities that are perceived by the mind and that these qualities do not exist in a material substance that exists outside the mind. He first argues that what are called the secondary qualities are like this, then he argues that what are called the primary qualities are also like this.

The first secondary quality that Philonous looks at is heat. According to Philonous, heat cannot exist outside the mind. Hylas, of course, argues that heat resides in a material substance and can exist outside the mind. However, Philonous points out that if we touch a very hot object, we will burn ourselves, and therefore, we will feel pain. Pain, of course, cannot exist without a mind to feel it, and a very hot oven — which Hylas would call a material substance — does not have a mind. Therefore, heat cannot exist without a mind.

Hylas objects to this reasoning by saying that heat and pain are two separate (distinct) sensations. However, Philonous responds by pointing out that when you place your hand in a fire, you don't perceive two separate sensations. Instead, you perceive both pain and heat at the same time. Since the fire affects you with both pain and heat at the same time, it follows that the two are one idea.

Philonous has another argument to make to support the idea that heat cannot exist outside the mind. Put one of your hands near a fire, and hold ice in the other hand. After a couple of minutes, drop the ice and place both of your hands in a bucket of room-temperature water. One hand will feel the water as warm; the other hand will feel the water as cold. If Hylas is correct, and heat and cold do exist in a material substance, then it would follow that the water in the bucket is both warm and cold at the same time. But, Philonous says, that is an absurdity. It makes much more sense to believe that heat and cold cannot exist outside the mind.

In addition, Philonous points out, if you prick your finger with a pin, you will feel pain, just as you would if you burn your finger with a hot coal from the fire. It doesn't make sense to think of the sensation of pain as existing in a pin, and so it doesn't make sense to think of the sensation of pain/heat as existing in a hot coal.

Hylas stops believing that heat and cold can exist without a mind to perceive them, and Philonous moves on to his argument that tastes cannot exist without a mind to perceive them. He states that tastes such as sweet and bitter are sensations. In particular, a sweet taste is a kind of pleasure, while a bitter taste is a kind of pain. Pleasure and pain are both things that are perceived by the mind, and it does not make sense to think that pleasure and pain reside in an unthinking material substance.

Once again, Hylas gives up his opinion; in this case, he stops thinking that tastes can exist without a mind to perceive them. Philonous also makes the argument that smells cannot exist without a mind to perceive them — it is similar to Philonous' other arguments.

Philonous also argues that sounds cannot exist without a mind to perceive them. Hylas argues that sounds reside in the air. As an example, Hylas points out if you strike a bell in a vacuum, the bell will make no sound; therefore, the sound must reside in the air.

However, Philonous argues that sound is a sensation — when the sound waves strike the ear, we hear a sound. Of course, if sound is a sensation, then it cannot exist without a mind to perceive it. So, Hylas admits, "I had as well grant that sounds, too, have no real being without the mind."

Philonous also argues that colors cannot exist without a mind to perceive them. Once again Hylas objects by saying that colors really reside in a material substance. However, Philonous points to some red and purple clouds (apparently, there is a beautiful sunset) and asks if the red and purple really reside in the clouds. Hylas answers, no, but then makes a distinction between real and apparent colors.

This distinction leads to problems. If some colors are real, and other colors are apparent, then how can we tell which colors are real and which colors are apparent? Suppose that we make a "most near and exact survey," as Hylas suggests. Would that work? Philonous points out that the "most near and exact survey" would be with a microscope, but that microscopes often reveal colors that we cannot see with the naked eye.

In addition, Philonous points out, the eyes of animals are often different from our eyes. For example, cats can see very well at night, but we can't. An example from the world of insects is that bees can perceive ultraviolet light, but we can't. It is possible that the colors these other beings see are different from the colors we see.

In addition, a person who suffers from jaundice sees everything as yellow. In twilight or in weak light, everything looks grey. Plus, a prism shows us that light that looks white is made up of many different colors. Once again, Hylas gives up his opinion and agrees with Philonous that colors cannot exist without a mind to perceive them.

So far, Philonous has been arguing that secondary qualities cannot exist outside the mind. Next, he begins to argue that primary qualities cannot exist without a mind to perceive them.

Philonous argues first that the primary qualities of extension and figure (shape) cannot exist outside the mind. To do so, he uses the same kind of arguments that he used to show that secondary qualities cannot exist without a mind to perceive them. He points out that one person will see something as "little, smooth, and round," while someone else sees it as "great, uneven, and angular."

For example, the world of a child is much different from that of an adult. To a child, things are much bigger than they appear to an adult. Even common table utensils such as a spoon and fork are large and unwieldy to a child.

In addition, things often look one way to the naked eye, but another way when seen under a microscope. To the naked eye, something may appear very smooth, but when looked at with a microscope, the same thing appears very rough.

Once again, Hylas gives up his belief that extension and figure (shape) reside in a material substance. He sees that he has to agree with Philonous that extension and figure (shape) cannot exist without a mind to perceive them.

Philonous then argues that solidity cannot exist without a mind to perceive it. By solidity we must either have no sensible quality in mind or we must have hardness or resistance in mind. If we have no sensible quality in mind, we can ignore solidity, because we are investigating sensible qualities.

However, if by solidity we have hardness or resistance in mind, then we must acknowledge that these qualities differ according to the minds that perceive them. What seems soft to one person may seem rough to another. A poor peasant who wears rags may think a certain piece of cloth soft, but a princess used to fine clothing may think the same piece of cloth is rough.

At this point Hylas objects, "I own that the very sensation of resistance, which is all you immediately perceive, is not in the *body*, but the cause of that sensation is."

To which Philonous replies, "But the causes of our sensations are not things immediately perceived, and therefore not sensible."

However, Hylas says that he finds it necessary to believe in a "material *substratum*," without which the qualities "cannot be conceived to exist." In addition, Hylas says that there are "two kinds of objects: the one perceived immediately, which are likewise called "ideas"; the other are real things or external objects, perceived by the mediation of ideas which are their images and representations."

However, according to Hylas, these real things or external objects are perceived by sense, although they are not immediately perceived. This surprises Philonous, who asks for an example of a thing that is perceived by the senses but is not immediately perceived. Hylas' example is a picture or statue of Julius Caesar. A person who sees a picture or statue of Julius Caesar is not immediately perceiving Julius Caesar, but when he sees a picture or statue of Julius Caesar, he nonetheless perceives Julius Caesar.

Philonous replies to the example by pointing out that all that is immediately perceived is some colors and a shape, and that this is all that a person who has never heard of Julius Caesar would perceive. A person who directs his thoughts to Julius Caesar after seeing the picture or statue does so only because of "reason and memory" and not because of perception. Therefore, we can continue to believe our original definition of sensible objects: "*sensible things are those only which are immediately perceived by sense.*"

And so our senses do not support belief in material substance or a material substratum. After all, as has been established earlier, we cannot perceive the cause of the sensations we perceive. If we are to conclude that material substance exists, it must be by the use of our reason.

Therefore, Philonous asks Hylas how he comes at his knowledge of material substance. Hylas is not able to answer, instead suggesting that Philonous must prove that material substance does not exist.

This is contrary to the usual rule of proof. If you believe that pink elephants exist and I do not, it is up to you to prove that pink elephants exist; it is not up to me to prove that they do not exist. The burden of proof lies on the person who makes the positive assertion (that something, such as material substance, exists), not on the person who makes the negative assertion (that something, such as material substance, does not exist).

But even granting that material substance exists, how are we to know which of the sensible qualities (ideas) we perceive will give us knowledge of that material substance? The color of an object varies. The shape of an object varies. (A chair's shape will vary as you view it from different angles.) The roughness or smoothness of an object varies according to the person who is perceiving the object. How are we to know which sensible quality truly represents the material substance?

Moreover, according to Hylas, material objects are themselves insensible but are perceived by their qualities (ideas). But this does not make sense to Philonous because it must mean that something that is sensible is like something that is insensible. This is similar to saying that something that is invisible is like a color.

Some Important Points

• As an empiricist, Berkeley believes that we acquire knowledge through the use of our senses. Since our senses do not show us that material substance exists, it must not exist. All the qualities we experience, we experience with the mind. Therefore, ultimate reality must be mental, not physical.

• To those who say that we perceive matter, Berkeley would reply that we do not. When I look at a desk, I see brownness and I see a certain shape. When I touch the desk, it feels hard and smooth. But all of these qualities are perceived by the mind. I perceive these sensible qualities, but I do not perceive anything called matter.

• Jay F. Rosenberg, in his book *The Practice of Philosophy*, writes about Berkeley's method of philosophical reasoning. (He's in favor of it.) See the sections "Lost Contrast" and "Emptiness" in the chapter titled "Five Ways to Criticize a Philosopher."

• Hylas believes in the existence of material objects; Philonous does not. In your opinion, which person is correct?

Note: The quotations by Berkeley that appear in this essay are from his book *Three Dialogues Between Hylas and Philonous*.

Chapter 4: Richard Taylor (1919-2003): Materialism and Personal Identity

In the second edition of his book *Metaphysics* (1974), Richard Taylor (1919-2003) examines the advantages and disadvantages of believing in the metaphysical theories of Materialism (in the form of the Identity Theory, aka the Identity Thesis) and of Dualism.

Materialism

Taylor describes the Identity Theory as the belief that I am a body only. I do not have an immaterial mind; I have only a material body. Thus, I am identical with my body. Whenever I talk about myself, I am really talking about my body.

As Taylor writes, "Now if my having a body consists simply in the identity of myself with my body, then it follows that I *am* body, and nothing more."

As you can see, the Identity Theory is a version of Materialism, the metaphysical theory that says that all reality is material, not mental; in other words, Materialism says that all reality consists of bodies, not minds.

The Identity Theory does have a great advantage in its simplicity. What makes up a person is not mysterious; a person is simply his body and nothing more.

Of course, this simplicity avoids the Mind-Body Problem that Dualism faces. According to Dualism, a person is composed of both a body and a mind, and the two interact with each other. For example, when my body is ill, it affects my ability to think clearly when taking a test. The interaction also works from mind to body. When my mind commands my arm to rise in the air when I want to answer a question that the teacher has asked, my arm will rise in the air (unless I am paralyzed or restrained).

However, this interaction of body and mind raises a problem: Since mind is immaterial and body is material, how can two such dissimilar things interact? Dualists have had a difficult time answering that question.

Materialism, however, does have a significant disadvantage. Suppose that we are identical with our body. We all know what happens to a person's body after the person dies: It decays. If the Identity Theory is true, it seems likely that we are mortal. When we die, our body decays and that is the end of us.

The Meaning of "Identity"

Taylor investigates what the Materialist means by "identity." He writes, "By 'identity' the [M]aterialist must mean a strict and total identity of himself and his body, nothing less."

But this leads to some interesting consequences. As Taylor writes, "Now to say of anything, X, and anything, Y, that X and Y are identical, or that they are really one and the same thing, one must be willing to assert of X whatever that he asserts of Y, and vice versa."

But are we willing to do that when we assert that I am identical with my body? I may be willing to say that I am morally blameworthy for something that I have done. Let's say that I cheated on a test. I can say that I am morally blameworthy, but can I say that my body is morally blameworthy? In addition:

1) I can say that I have a wish (for example, I wish to meet my favorite TV actress), but can I say that my body has a wish?

2) I can say that I am religious, but can I say that my body is religious?

3) I can say that I am in love, but can I say that my body is in love?

In addition, Taylor points out, the Materialist's definition of "identity" will have problems when it comes to epistemological predicates. For example, suppose that someone is mistaken about something. In Taylor's example, someone mistakenly believes that today is February 31. Now if this person is mistaken, and if the Identity Theory is true, it must be the case that his body is mistaken, which certainly seems odd.

In Taylor's words: "Thus, if I believe something — believe, for instance, that today is February 31 — then I am in a certain state; the state, namely, of having a certain belief which is in this case necessarily a false one. Now how can a physical state of any physical object be identical with that? And how, in particular, can anything be a *false* physical state of an object? ... A physiologist might give a complete physical description of a brain and nervous system at a particular time, but he could never distinguish some of those states as true and others as false, nor would he have any idea what to look for if he were asked to do this. At least, so it would certainly seem."

Platonic Dualism

Platonic Dualism is the view that a person is a soul or mind that has the use of a body. The soul or mind is the real, essential part of the person, and the soul or mind will live on after the person's body dies. This view is very congenial to many religious people, as it is consistent with their religious beliefs. For example, immortality is central to the Christian faith, and Platonic Dualism supports a belief in immortality.

Platonic Dualism also has other advantages. Human beings wish to think of themselves as being "something more than just one more item of matter in the world," and Platonic Dualism allows them to do that. In addition, Platonic Dualism avoids the pitfalls of Materialism.

However, as Taylor points out, Platonic Dualism has problems of its own. We can ask how the soul is related to the body. Does the soul possess the body? Possession, however, is a social and a legal term. We possess the things we own, but do we possess our body? A person can own a slave, but the slave still possesses his own body "in a metaphysical sense in which it could not possibly be the body of his master."

We can also ask this: Does the soul occupy the body? But occupancy is a term that is a physical concept, and since the soul or mind is not physical, we cannot use this term to describe the relationship between the mind or soul, and the body.

And, of course, there is the problem of how the mind and body interact: the Mind-Body Problem.

Note: The quotations by Taylor that appear in this essay are from his book *Metaphysics* (2nd edition, 1974).

Chapter 5: Ludwig Wittgenstein (1889-1951): Philosophical Investigations

Ludwig Wittgenstein (1889-1951) had much to say on the subject of language and metaphysics. In his *Philosophical Investigations*, which was posthumously published in 1953, his views on language (which had been greatly revised since the publication of his *Tractatus Logico-Philosophicus* in London in 1922) were published.

According to Wittgenstein, a study of the ordinary use of language — that is, a study of the way people who are not philosophers ordinarily use language — is very important. Such a study can solve — or dissolve — many philosophical problems that arise out of a misuse of language. As you can tell, Wittgenstein greatly influenced what are called the ordinary-language philosophers.

In his study, Wittgenstein concluded that language is a game. As such, it follows rules. There are many different forms of language-games, and new language-games can come into existence and old language-games can pass out of existence. Language has many purposes, and each purpose is a language-game.

A language-game that is still in existence is the giving of orders. A mason can point to a piece of stone and say "slab" to an assistant, and the assistant will bring that particular piece of stone to the mason. By saying a single word, the mason was giving an order to his or her assistant.

Other language-games that are currently in use include these:

"Describing the appearance of an object, or giving its measurements —

"Constructing an object from a description (a drawing) —
"Reporting an event —
"Speculating about an event — "

And many more.

One thing to notice here is that each language game has its own rules. A philosopher — or anyone else — will run into problems if he or she ignores the rules of a particular language-game. For example: You can give an order to your assistant, but you should not give an order to your boss.

Such mistakes can be made if one supposes that all language-games are similar. They are not. A particular language-game will be similar to some language-games, but it will be different from other language-games. There is no feature that is common to all language-games.

To illustrate this, Wittgenstein asks us to think of games. There are many different kinds of games: "board-games, card-games, ball-games, Olympic games, and so on." However, there is no feature that is common to all games. Some games involve more than one player; others do not. Some games have a winner; others do not. Some games involve competition; others do not.

What these games do have is what Wittgenstein likens to "family resemblances." The members of a family need not have one certain feature in common. Some members can have Grandpa's eyes; other members can have Grandma's nose; still other members can have another feature in common. However, although there is no one particular feature shared by all the members of a family, you can look at the members of a family and tell that they are all members of the same family.

Language-games also have family resemblances with each other. There is no one particular feature that the various language-games have in common, but nonetheless the various language-games have family resemblances.

Wittgenstein believes that philosophers sometimes create problems by ignoring the rules that govern the use of the words they are incorrectly using. When this happens, Wittgenstein says, the words the philosophers are incorrectly using are "language on a holiday."

Therefore, Wittgenstein says, when a philosopher uses a certain word, the philosopher needs to ask him- or herself, "[I]s the word ever actually used in this way in the language-game which is its original home?" If philosophers would only do this consistently, many philosophical problems would disappear.

For example, one philosophical problem is that of free will versus determinism. According to the determinists, Humankind does not have free will. Whenever we make a decision, we are making the decision in accordance with the kind of character we have.

Let's say that I have decided to attend class today. (One quarter I did not miss any classes and received straight A's on my report card!) A determinist would say that my character made me decide not to miss class today. Further, the determinist would say that my character was created by heredity and environment. I was born with a high IQ, and I grew up in a household filled with books. (I recommend that if a suitable occasion arises you always tell other people that you have a high IQ — lie if you have to.) Since my heredity and environment are beyond my control (I did not choose to be born, and if I had chosen to be born, I would have picked richer parents — just kidding, Mom and Dad), I am not free. Whatever I choose to do, such as attending my class today, is not the result of a free act — it is the result of conditions beyond my control. Therefore, I am not free.

But if we take a look at the way we ordinarily use the word "free," instead of using the specialized meaning that the philosophers have given the word, we can dissolve the philosophical problem of free will versus determinism. By my being free to choose to go to my class today, we mean that no one is preventing me from going to my class. So, unless someone kidnaps me and forcibly takes me to a bar, I am free to attend class.

We can criticize this ordinary-language method of philosophizing. Other professions have created a necessary but specialized jargon — as you can tell by eavesdropping on a physician or lawyer. Why shouldn't philosophers also have a specialized vocabulary as long as they are careful to define their terms? And does ordinary language really solve the philosophical problem of free will versus determinism?

Back to Wittgenstein and his ideas. Wittgenstein wants his investigation of language "to bring words back from their metaphysical to their ordinary use." If he is successful at doing this, then he will have cleared up philosophical language — that is, language that has erected "houses of cards."

These "houses of cards" and philosophical problems in general arise from a failure to use words correctly, according to Wittgenstein. If philosophers did use words as the words were meant to be used, no philosophical problems would arise.

In fact, Wittgenstein writes, "A philosophical problem has the form: 'I don't know my way about.'" But if the philosopher knew how to use words correctly, then he would know his way about them and would be able to dissolve the philosophical problem. If Wittgenstein had his way, all philosophers would use words clearly and accurately.

Wittgenstein wrote, "For the clarity that we are aiming at is indeed *complete* clarity. But this simply means that the philosophical problems should *completely* disappear."

When that happens, students presumably will no longer be required to take tests on metaphysics.

Note: The quotations by Wittgenstein that appear in this essay are from his *Philosophical Investigations*, translated by G. E. M. Anscombe.

Chapter 6: David Bruce (born 1954): Metaphysical Theories' Strengths and Weaknesses

One good way to choose among competing metaphysical theories is to list their strengths and weaknesses, and then choose on that basis.

MATERIALISM

Materialism is the view that all reality consists of matter. Thus, the only things that are real are empty space, physical (that is, material) objects, and energy. Epicurus is a Materialist.

Strengths

One strength of Materialism is that it is the view presupposed by modern science. Scientists assume that there is a cause for everything that happens. In addition, scientists assume that the cause naturally occurs in the universe. Thus, if we get ill, scientists look for a reason why we became ill; for example, a virus or a cancer. Obviously, science has been very successful — we owe many wonderful inventions to scientists. However, scientists — in investigating the universe — assume that transcendental entities such as God or minds don't exist. (Of course, some scientists believe in God, but they would agree that to say "a miracle occurred" is a poor explanation of the results of an experiment.)

Another strength of Materialism is that most of us assume that an external physical world exists. We are accustomed to speak of physical objects as opposed to the objects we only dream about. Materialism does a good job of explaining physical phenomena.

Weaknesses

A weakness of Materialism is that it does a poor job of explaining mental phenomena such as wanting, thinking, dreaming, etc. After all, there is a difference in the way that I feel something and in the way that I observe you feel something. When I have an earache, I really feel it. When you have an earache, I see you hold your hand on your ear and I hear you moan, but I don't feel the earache. Why is there is a difference in the pain I experience and in the pain I observe you experiencing? After all, according to the Materialists, the only thing that exists is matter and both of us are physical objects. How can something that is only a physical object experience pain or a dream, or make a wish?

Another weakness of Materialism is that it pretty much shuts the door on the idea of our being immortal. After all, we know what happens to our body after we die — it decays. I suppose that a god could reassemble our scattered atoms and bring us to life again, but then that kind of god would transcend matter and according to Materialism, no such transcendent being exists. (In the Christian religion, St. Paul believed that we would be resurrected; in the afterlife, each of us will have what he called a spiritual body.)

IDEALISM

Idealism is the view that all reality consists of minds and ideas. Objects are not physical; instead, they are bundles of ideas that are perceived by minds. George Berkeley is an Idealist.

Strengths

A strength of Idealism is that it does a good job of explaining mental phenomena such as wanting, thinking, dreaming, etc. After all, we are minds and everything that exists is a bundle of ideas that we perceive. Of course, Idealists can account for wanting, thinking, dreaming, etc.

Another strength of Idealism is that it is possible that we are immortal. Perhaps our mind will live on although the bundle of ideas we call our body disintegrates.

Weaknesses

A weakness of Idealism is that we need to ask how objects stay in existence when they are not perceived. After all, according to George Berkeley, to be is to be perceived. Therefore, if no one is in my office to perceive the office furniture, does that mean that the office furniture ceases to exist? Berkeley came up with the theory that God perceives everything; therefore, everything stays in existence even when no one is around to see it.

Another problem with Idealism is that it finds it difficult to account for our knowledge of our own minds. David Hume, who was an empiricist, believed that all that is perceived by us is a flow of sensations, thoughts, and memories, but that a mental substance called a mind is not perceived by us. Therefore, why should we believe that we have a mind that is a mental substance? Berkeley criticized belief in material substance, but Hume used the same kind of arguments to criticize belief in mental substance.

DUALISM

Dualism is the view that all reality consists of both minds and bodies. Therefore, a human being has a body but also has a mind or soul. Both René Descartes and Plato are Dualists.

Strengths

A strength of Dualism is that, as Richard Taylor points out, it avoids the problems of the Identity Theory (the Materialist theory that we are identical with our body). One problem with the Identity Theory is that we can't say the same things about our mind and body. For example, we can say "my mind has a wish," but it is absurd to say "my body has a wish." Or we can say, "I am religious," but it is absurd to say, "my body is religious."

Also, in our minds we sometimes make mistakes. In the second edition of his book titled *Metaphysics*, Richard Taylor uses the example of thinking that today is February 31, and then asks:

> Now how can a physical state of any physical object be identical with that? And how, in particular, can anything be a *false* physical state of an object? The physical states of things, it would seem, just *are*, and one cannot even think of anything that could ever distinguish one such state from another as being either true or false. A physiologist might give a complete physical description of a brain and nervous system at a particular time, but he could never distinguish some of those states as true and the others as false, nor would he have any idea what to look for if he were asked to do this. At least, so it would certainly seem.

Another strength of Dualism is that we experience so much of the world in terms of having a mind and a body. They are concepts that we are comfortable with and use in our language.

A third strength of Dualism is that it is possible we are immortal: Our mind may survive the deaths of our body.

Weaknesses

The major weakness of Dualism is the mind-body problem. If we are both mind and body, then how do our mind and body interact? After all, the body is material, while the mind is immaterial, so how can one affect the other? If I try to use my mind to move an object such as a pencil off the floor, the pencil won't budge until I lean down and pick it up with my fingers. How can my mind tell my body to move? And how can my body interact with my mind?

A weakness with Dualism is stating how the mind is related to the body. "Possession" is a social and legal term, so we can't say that the mind possesses the body. In addition, "occupy" is a physical term, so we can't say that the mind occupies the body.

CONCLUSION

I leave it up to the reader to decide whether Materialism, Idealism, or Dualism is the correct metaphysical theory.

EPISTEMOLOGY

Chapter 7: Plato (427?-347 B.C.E.): The Visible and the Invisible

Plato (427?-347 B.C.E.) is one of the giants of philosophy. Part of his accomplishment was to create a complete philosophical system, one whose parts — metaphysics, epistemology, ethics, political and social philosophy, etc. — were closely integrated. Philosopher Alfred North Whitehead once said, "The safest general characterization of the European philosophical tradition is that it consists of a series of footnotes to Plato" (*Process and Reality*, p. 39 [Free Press, 1979].

In Plato's description of the Divided Line in Book 6 of *The Republic*, we see how closely his metaphysics and epistemology are related. (Search online for an illustration of the Divided Line.) According to Plato, reality has various levels. Corresponding to each level of reality is a level of knowledge. Plato (the main speaker in *The Republic* is actually Socrates, but most scholars think that Plato is actually expressing his own ideas) asks the reader to imagine a line and to divide it into two unequal parts. Then the reader is asked to take the two parts of the line and divide each of them into two unequal parts. Each of the parts of the line will correspond to different levels of reality, and knowledge of the different levels of reality will correspond to different levels of knowledge.

The first division that we make in the line corresponds to two different major levels of reality. There is the visible order of reality: We see the world we live in and also see images in mirrors and reflections on pools of water. Then there is the invisible order of reality: This is the realm of numbers, geometrical objects such as squares and triangles, and abstract concepts such as equality and justice. As we will see later, Plato believed that the invisible order of reality is more real than the visible order.

Each of the two orders of reality has been divided into two sections. This essay will describe Plato's view of reality, beginning with what is less real and ending with what is most real.

Imagining

The bottom half of the divided line is devoted to the visible order. The bottom half of the part of the divided line that is devoted to the visible order is the part of reality that consists of images. These images include shadows and reflections in water or on other surfaces — for example, a mirror.

All of these images are a very low order of reality. When we know about images, we have the degree of knowledge that Plato calls **imagining**. Images are less real than the objects that belong to the next level of reality.

Belief

The top half of the part of the line that is devoted to the visible order is the part of reality that consists of physical objects. These objects include animals, all plants, and the whole class of objects made by Humankind. In addition, these objects include individual trees and individual human beings.

All of these physical objects are still a very low order of reality, according to Plato. When we know about physical objects, we have the degree of knowledge that Plato calls **belief**. Physical objects are less real than the objects that belong to the next level of reality — the level of reality that is the bottom half of the level of reality known as the intelligible order.

Understanding

The top half of the divided line is devoted to the intelligible order. The bottom half of the part of the divided line that is devoted to the intelligible order is the part of reality that consists of objects of geometry and kindred objects. These objects include triangles, squares, circles, and numbers. By a triangle, I don't mean a triangle that is drawn on a chalkboard — I mean the geometrical object that is called a triangle. The triangle that is drawn on a chalkboard is not a perfect triangle — it does not have straight lines; a geometrical triangle (the triangle that you study in geometry class) is a perfect triangle and does have perfectly straight lines. Indeed, the triangle that is drawn on the chalkboard in a classroom is only an image of a real triangle — the perfect triangle with perfectly straight lines.

All of these geometrical objects are a high order of reality — but they are not the highest level. When we know about geometrical and mathematical objects, we have the degree of knowledge that Plato calls **understanding**. However, geometrical and mathematical objects are still less real than the objects that belong to the next level of reality.

To investigate the objects of geometry, we start with assumptions that are arbitrary starting points. People who study Euclid's geometry will start by learning axioms — the assumptions of his geometry. If you reject Euclid's axioms and come up with your own, you can establish a non-Euclidean geometry.

Intelligence

The top half of the part of the line that is devoted to the visible order is the part of reality that consists of the Forms or Ideas. The Forms are the highest form of reality. They are eternal and unchanging. Plato believed that there were many Forms. There is a Form for Tree, of which individual physical trees are only images. There is also a Form for Human Being and Forms for other physical objects. In addition, there are Forms for Beauty, Truth, Justice, Excellence, Piety, etc.

The Forms are the highest level of reality — they are what is most real — but the highest Form of all is the Form of the Good. When we know about the Forms, we have the degree of knowledge that Plato calls **intelligence**.

To investigate the Forms, we use dialectic. We start with an assumption, then subject the assumption to a rigorous process of analysis. This is what Socrates does in Platonic dialogue after Platonic dialogue. By investigating assumptions about the Form of Piety, we can acquire knowledge about the Form of Piety itself.

The Allegory of the Cave

One of the most famous allegories in Western civilization is Plato's Allegory of the Cave, which also appears in *The Republic* — at the beginning of Book 7. The allegory represents Plato's views about metaphysics and epistemology.

In the allegory, Plato asks us to imagine a strange scenario. A group of people has been kept imprisoned in a cave all their lives. They are tied up and are facing a wall. Behind the prisoners is a fire. Between the fire and the prisoners is a raised way on which a low wall has been built. People walk on the raised way, but they are hidden by the wall. However, they carry objects above them — statues of men and animals, etc. The shadows of these objects are cast in front of the prisoners.

Imagining

All the prisoners have ever seen in their lives are these shadows, and this is what they think reality consists of. The prisoners have the degree of knowledge that Plato calls **imagining**, and the level of reality that they understand is that of images.

Belief

But suppose that a prisoner got free and turned and saw the raised way and the men walking along the raised way. This prisoner would have reached a higher level of understanding — that of **belief**. This prisoner would understand the level of reality that consists of physical objects.

Understanding

Suppose further that the prisoner is taken outside of the cave. In the beginning, the light of the sun would hurt his eyes and he would not be able to see much. Plato writes that at first the man could most easily see shadows and the reflections of men and of other things that are reflected in water. In the allegory, these shadows and reflections correspond to geometrical and mathematical objects. When the prisoner reached an understanding of the shadows and reflections outside the cave, he would have reached the level of knowledge called **understanding**, and he would understand the level of reality that consists of geometrical and mathematical objects.

Intelligence

After a while, the prisoner's eyes would grow accustomed to the light and he would then see the physical objects outside the cave: individual human beings, individual trees, etc. In the allegory, these physical objects outside the cave correspond to the Forms: the Form of Human Being, the Form of Tree, the Form of Piety, etc.

But later, the prisoner's eyes would have grown so accustomed to the light that he could look at the Sun. In the allegory, the Sun represents the Form of the Good. When the prisoner is able to look at the Sun, he would understand the Form of the Good.

When the prisoner reached an understanding of the trees and human beings outside the cave, and of the Sun itself, he would have reached the level of knowledge called **intelligence**, and he would understand the level of reality that consists of the Forms, including the Form of the Good.

Back to the Cave

Suppose further that the prisoner returned to the cave and tried to tell the other prisoners what he had seen. He would be confused by the darkness of the cave, and the other prisoners would not believe his story. In addition, if the prisoner were to try to free the other prisoners and lead them out of the cave, the other prisoners would kill him. In Plato's words, "If [the prisoners] could lay hands on the man who was trying to set them free and lead them up, they would kill him."

Levels of Interpretation

The Allegory of the Cave can be interpreted in many ways. One interpretation is the one we have been looking at: The allegory explains Plato's views on metaphysics and epistemology.

Another interpretation is that the allegory explains why Socrates was killed by his fellow Athenians. Socrates escaped from the cave, but returned to become a stinging fly to his fellow Athenians in an attempt to lead them out of the cave. The Athenians resented Socrates' efforts and so killed him.

In addition, the allegory explains what philosophy is and what the philosopher does. The philosopher is attempting to get out of the cave by educating him- or herself about the various levels of reality — especially the highest level of reality: the Forms.

The Allegory of the Cave can also be interpreted as a criticism of our pre-philosophic lives. If all we are concerned about is the acquisition of money, then we are at the level of watching shadows on a wall.

Other interpretations exist, and more than one interpretation can be held simultaneously. The Allegory of the Cave is a work of high literary and philosophical merit, and as such, each generation of Humankind discovers that it says something to them.

Note: The quotations by Plato that appear in this essay are from his book *Republic*, translated by F. M. Cornford.

Chapter 8: René Descartes (1596-1650): Meditations

René Descartes (1596-1650) lived in an age of skepticism. The New Science had grown to be very important, and it had brought into question many of the beliefs that had been held by the Church. For example, the Church had believed that the Earth is at the center of the universe, and that the Sun orbits around the Earth. However, the Polish astronomer Copernicus (1473-1543) became famous for his heliocentric theory that stated that the Sun is at the center of the solar system and that the Earth orbits around the Sun. Other scientists such as the Italian astronomer Galileo (1564-1642) believed in the Copernican theory. Many people were unsure what to believe: what the Church told them, or what the scientists told them.

Descartes was also aware that philosophy finds it difficult to come up with definitive answers to its perennial questions. (Of course, if a definitive answer could be found to a philosophical question, the issue would no longer be philosophical, and philosophers would move on to other questions.) Despite his excellent education by the Jesuits (who are known for providing excellent educations), Descartes found himself wracked by doubt.

Because of his aversion to skepticism (the position that knowledge is impossible to acquire), Descartes made it his life's work to put philosophy on a firm foundation. In fact, Descartes wanted to find something that is impossible to doubt — that is, something that cannot be doubted — to serve as the basis for his philosophy.

Methodic Doubt

To conquer his doubt, Descartes decided to use methodic doubt. He would doubt everything that could possibly be doubted until he discovered something that could not be doubted. This would be the firm foundation for philosophy for which he was searching.

Doubting the Senses

To begin his methodic doubt, Descartes focused on his senses: seeing, hearing, touching, smelling, and tasting. He discovered that his senses were unreliable. For one thing, we are fooled by optical illusions. Square towers, when seen from a distance, look round. Large people, when seen from a distance, look small. In addition, Descartes points out, he has often dreamed that he was awake. While dreaming, he thought he was awake, and it was not until he woke up that he discovered his error. So even while writing the lines people still read hundreds of years after they were written, Descartes believed that he could doubt that he was awake.

Doubting Mathematics

Next in his methodic doubt, Descartes doubts such truths as that 2 + 3 = 5, and that squares have four sides. You may object: Surely these things are true whether I am sleeping or not. Perhaps not, Descartes replies, because for all I know, there may be a deceiving demon who makes me think up is down, and square is round. So perhaps 2 + 3 really equals 6, and perhaps a square is really a circle. The deceiving demon may be making me think false things are true. (This device of the deceiving demon shows just how seriously Descartes took his methodic doubt; he really did want to discover something that it was *impossible* to doubt.)

Cogito Ergo Sum

Having doubted all these things, Descartes now discovers something that it is impossible to doubt. And that is that he is doubting — as well as thinking, affirming, denying, wishing, and other intellectual activities. And if he is doubting, he must exist in order to be doubting. Therefore, Descartes writes: *Cogito ergo sum.* This is Latin for "I think, therefore I am." This is the thing that cannot be doubted, even if there is a deceiving demon around. After all, if the deceiving demon deceives me, I must exist in order to be deceived. As Descartes writes, "I am, I exist — that is certain...."

What Kind of Thing am I?

So Descartes knows that he exists, but he then asks what kind of thing is he. His answer is that he is a thinking thing. Descartes performs a large number of intellectual activities: He doubts, he thinks, he wishes, he understands, he conceives, etc. Because of these things, Descartes says that he is a thinking thing.

In his other *Meditations*, Descartes goes on to show that he also has a body (and that God and physical objects exist). Descartes is a Dualist: He believes that he consists of two things:

1) an immaterial mind, which thinks and which is not extended in space, and

2) a material body, which is extended in space.

Since Descartes first established the existence of the mind, then the existence of the body, he felt that human beings consist of two different things.

The Wax Example

In addition to being a Dualist, Descartes was a Rationalist. As such, he believed that knowledge is acquired from the use of our reason, not our senses. As we have already seen, our senses frequently deceive us. To show that we acquire knowledge by the use of our reason, Descartes asks us to think about a piece of beeswax.

So imagine that you have a piece of beeswax fresh from a hive. What do your senses tell you about the beeswax?

- You can taste the honey that was stored in the beeswax.

- You can smell the flowers visited by the bees that made the beeswax and the honey.

- You can see the color, shape, and size of the beeswax.

- You can feel the coldness and the hardness of the beeswax.

- You can hear a sound if you rap on the beeswax.

In short, all your senses tell you that this is a piece of beeswax freshly taken from the hive.

But next imagine that you put the piece of beeswax close to a fire so that the fire heats the beeswax. What do your senses then tell you about the piece of beeswax?

- The taste of the honey has vanished.
- The odor of flowers has vanished.
- The beeswax changes color.
- The beeswax loses its shape.

- The beeswax increases in size.
- The beeswax becomes liquid.
- The beeswax grows hot.
- If you rap on the beeswax, it gives out no sound.

In short, the sensory information received from the piece of beeswax brought close to a fire is completely different from the sensory information received from the piece of beeswax before it was brought close to a fire.

If we were to gain knowledge only from our senses, we would have to conclude that the cold beeswax and the hot beeswax were two completely different substances, because this is what our senses tell us. But of course, we realize that the cold beeswax and the hot beeswax are both the same substance: beeswax. Therefore, Descartes says, it is our reason — not our senses — that tells us that the cold beeswax and the hot beeswax are the same substance.

In addition, we use our reason to conclude that the people we see walking in the street are really people. From my third-story office window, all I *see* are colored images moving on the street. For all I know, the colored images are really nothing more than ghosts or robots, but my reason concludes that the moving color images are people because whenever I walk on the street, I meet people and not ghosts or robots. Once again, reason — not the senses — gives us knowledge.

Because of these things, Descartes concluded that the real source of knowledge is reason, not the senses. Descartes is therefore a Rationalist and not an Empiricist.

Conclusion: My Favorite Descartes Joke

Descartes was flying on an old-fashioned plane that has propellers. As you may know, if the propellers are turning at the right speed, they will look as if they have stopped although they are really going very fast. A fellow passenger looked out the window at the propellers, then tapped Descartes on the shoulder and asked, "Excuse me, but are those propellers moving?" Descartes looked out the window, and replied, "I think not."

Then he disappeared.

Note: The quotations by Descartes that appear in this essay are from his book *Meditations*, translated by Laurence J. Lafleur.

Chapter 9: David Hume (1711-1776): Skeptical Doubts

David Hume (1711-1776) is Scotland's greatest philosopher. As such, he is in the tradition of the great British Empiricists, who include John Locke (1632-1704) and George Berkeley (1685-1753). As an Empiricist, Hume believed that the source of all our knowledge about the world comes from the senses. Hume is opposed to the Rationalists, whose ranks include Plato (427?-347 B.C.E.) and Descartes (1596-1650). The Rationalists believe that the source of all our knowledge is reason.

According to Hume, there are two kinds of objects of human reason. The first is "relations of ideas," which is the kind of knowledge that mathematics, including geometry, algebra, and arithmetic, have. This kind of knowledge includes, in Hume's words, "every affirmation which is either intuitively or demonstratively certain."

Examples of relations of ideas include such facts as 3 + 2 = 5 from arithmetic, and the Pythagorean Theorem (*"the square of the hypotenuse is equal to the squares of the two sides"*) from geometry. This kind of knowledge is absolutely certain and does not come from sense experience. Sentences of relations of ideas are today called analytic sentences.

The second kind of object of human reason is "matters of fact." This kind of knowledge is completely empirical, being the knowledge that we gain by using our five senses: seeing, hearing, touching, tasting, and smelling. A sentence such as "The sun is shining" represents a matter of fact if you look at the sky and indeed see that the sun is shining.

These two kinds of knowledge are very different. Knowledge of "relations of ideas" is *a priori* knowledge, which means that we arrive at it by using our reason and not our senses. *A priori* means prior to experience. Knowledge of "matters of fact" is *a posteriori* knowledge, which means that we arrive at it by using our senses. *A posteriori* means after (posterior to) experience.

Hume believed that "relations of ideas" tell us nothing about the world. After all, in the physical universe, there are no perfect squares or triangles. In addition, no one has ever seen a "one" or a "two," although you may have seen one apple or the number "1" (which is a symbol) written on a chalkboard.

Therefore, Hume is an Empiricist because he believed that all our information about the world comes from the senses.

This leads us to a question. Can we extend our knowledge beyond mere relations of ideas and matters of fact? Relations of ideas give us facts about abstract ideas (for example, $2 + 2 = 4$). Matters of fact give us facts about the world (the sky is blue today). Is there any way in which we can go beyond these kinds of knowledge?

That is something that science attempts to do. On the basis of empirical facts, scientists attempt to derive principles that can be used to extend our knowledge. For example, the scientists who are physicians have discovered the principle that diseases have causes; in other words, there is a reason why someone catches a disease.

For example, you may suffer from cavities because of eating too many sweets and not brushing often enough after meals. Here's another example: a lack of iodine in a person's diet may cause a goiter (a swelling of the thyroid gland).

Because of his belief in the principle of causality, Jonas Salk studied polio until he was able to invent a vaccine that would prevent people from being afflicted with polio.

Modern science is based largely on the principle of causality. If astronomers look at a planet and see that it wobbles, they may conclude that it is affected by the gravity of an unseen planet. They reason that the wobble (the effect) occurs because of the gravity of another planet (the cause). On the basis of the principle of causality, astronomers concluded that Pluto must exist before they ever observed it.

According to Hume, "All reasonings concerning matter of fact seem to be founded on the relation of *cause* and *effect*." As a philosopher concerned with how we acquire knowledge, Hume decided to investigate the principle of causality. After all, according to Hume, only by reasoning about cause and effect can we "go beyond the evidence of our memory and senses."

Hume therefore performs a thought experiment. He asks you to suppose that an intelligent person is suddenly brought into the world, then Hume asks, what would that person — at first — observe? Such a person, although intelligent, would simply observe objects and events. One event would happen, then another, then another, etc. But the person would not immediately be able to arrive at the concept of cause and effect.

Newborn infants, some of whom are very intelligent (just ask any mother), go through the same thing. Set an infant in front of a mirror for the first time and it won't understand that it is looking at its own reflection.

After a while, that intelligent person will arrive at the concept of cause and effect. Why? Certainly not because the intelligent person has seen causality. Causality is not the kind of thing that anyone can see. All we see is one event happening, then another, etc. But no one has ever seen causality; that is, no one has ever seen a *necessary connection* between events.

Let's say that our intelligent — and now experienced — person sees snow. Immediately he associates the idea of coldness with the snow. But why does he do that? According to Hume, "he has not, by all his experience, acquired any idea or knowledge of the secret power by which the one object produces the other, nor is it by any process of reasoning he is engaged to draw this inference ...."

So why does he associate snow with coldness? Hume's answer is "*custom* or *habit*." The intelligent person has experienced snow on a number of occasions, and each time the snow has been cold, and therefore by habit the person associates snow with coldness. But the intelligent person has never seen a necessary connection between snow and coldness.

What the intelligent person does see are these things:

1) Constant conjunction: Each time the intelligent person picks up a snowball, he or she feels a cold sensation, and

2) Temporal priority: First the intelligent person picks up a snowball, and then he or she feels a cold sensation.

However, the intelligent person does not see a necessary connection between snow and coldness — or between flame and heat, for that matter. Without a necessary connection, we can have no knowledge of causality.

According to Hume, all inferences from experience (for example, the inference that snow is cold) are "effects of custom, not of reasoning." The intelligent person picks up one snowball, finds that it is cold, then picks up another snowball, finds that it is also cold, etc. After experiencing several snowballs, the intelligent person concludes that snowballs are cold.

The same thing applies to the game of pool. We use a cue stick to hit the cue ball against a colored ball. Through custom or habit, we expect the cue ball to hit a colored ball and make it move. But according to Hume, this is something we expect *only* through custom or habit. Our senses do not detect a necessary connection between the movement of the cue ball and the movement of a colored ball.

Instead, we hit a cue ball against a colored ball and the colored ball moves, and then we hit a cue ball against another colored ball and once again the colored ball moves, etc. Eventually, we expect that whenever we hit a cue ball against a colored ball that the colored ball will move.

But is that the way reason works? According to Hume, no. A geometer does not work with one circle, then another circle, then yet another circle, etc., until he concludes something. No. All the geometer has to do is work with one circle. A theorem that applies to one circle will apply to all circles, and so there is no need for the geometer to work with many circles.

In Hume's words, "The conclusions which [reason] draws considering one circle are the same which it would form upon surveying all the circles in the universe. But no man, having seen only one body move after being impelled by another, could infer that every other body will move after a like impulse. All inferences from reasoning, therefore, are effects of custom, not of reasoning."

If Hume is right, his reasoning would have a great effect upon Humankind. By doing away with the principle of causality, he has removed the prop of modern science. Without the principle of causality, we would not know what would happen if we were to crack a chicken egg to make an omelet. The chicken egg might explode like a scene in a Sylvester Stallone movie; it might pour forth beautiful music, it might turn into a beautiful woman or an ugly prince, or a solid gold egg might be inside.

When a philosophical theory appears to contradict common sense, we need to take a close look at that philosophical theory. Hume has used empirical reasoning and shown that it denies that we can have knowledge of causes and effects. Perhaps by showing us this consequence of Empiricism, Hume has shown that Empiricism is incorrect. Perhaps reason does make a contribution to knowledge.

The philosopher Immanuel Kant (1724-1804) will attempt to forge a compromise between Empiricism and Rationalism. He will argue that both the senses and reason have a contribution to make to knowledge.

Note: The quotations by Hume that appear in this essay are from his book *An Enquiry Concerning Human Understanding.*

Chapter 10: Immanuel Kant (1724-1804): Two Sources of Knowledge

In his important book *Critique of Pure Reason*, Immanuel Kant (1724-1804) wrote about the sources of human knowledge. In the *Critique of Pure Reason*, Kant attempted to forge a compromise between the Rationalists and the Empiricists by showing that both reason and the senses contribute to human knowledge.

In so doing, Kant wants to be able to claim for human beings a kind of knowledge that is necessary (a statement is necessary if it is impossible to deny it), yet tells us about the world. The Rationalists, whose kind of knowledge is represented by mathematics and geometry, have knowledge that is necessary but that does not tell us about the world. For example, the Pythagorean Theorem is necessary, but it does not tell us about the world because there are no perfect triangles in the material universe.

On the other hand, the Empiricists, whose knowledge comes from the senses, have knowledge that tells us about the world but that is not necessary. For example, I may think that I am typing away at my computer right now, but the Rationalist Descartes would point out that I may be mistaken — I may actually be in bed dreaming that I am typing away at my computer. Another example: I may think that the world has turned different shades of yellow overnight, but although this is what my senses tell me, I may actually be suffering from jaundice, a disease in which the sufferer sees only different shades of yellow.

The Distinction Between *A Priori* and *A Posteriori* Knowledge

According to Kant, "There can be no doubt that all our knowledge begins with experience. ... But though all our knowledge begins with experience, it does not follow that it all arises out of experience."

That is Kant's thesis statement. In giving evidence to support his analysis of knowledge, Kant used several terms that we will have to define. Among these are the terms *a priori* and *a posteriori*.

A priori knowledge is completely independent of sensory experience. Here are some examples of *a priori* statements:

- $2 + 3 = 5$.

- The square of the hypotenuse is equal to the squares of the two sides (the Pythagorean Theorem).

- A thing is equivalent to itself; that is, A is equivalent to A.

- $2 + 3 = 3 + 2$.

As you can see, mathematical and geometric knowledge is *a priori* knowledge. This is knowledge that is completely independent of sensory experience.

A posteriori knowledge is knowledge that is wholly empirical; that is, knowledge that we learn from our five senses. Here are some examples of *a posteriori* statements:

- There is a lightning storm outside.

- The grass is green.

- The basketball team from Ohio University in Athens, Ohio, wears green and white uniforms.

- There is a Wendy's in my hometown.

As you can see, *a posteriori* knowledge is completely derived from the senses.

The Distinction Between Analytic and Synthetic Judgments

Kant also makes a distinction between analytic and synthetic judgments. By "judgments," Kant means what we today call "propositions." A proposition is a statement that affirms or denies something and that is true or false. Examples of propositions include "All bachelors are male" and "The grass is green."

An analytic statement is one in which the predicate is contained in the subject. For example, the statement "All bachelors are male" is an analytic statement. Since "bachelor" means "unmarried male," the predicate "are male" adds no new information to the subject "All bachelors."

The strength of analytic statements is their necessity — meaning it is not possible to deny them. Since the predicate is contained in the subject, analytic statements are necessary. The weakness of analytic statements is that they don't tell us anything new — the predicate merely conveys an idea that is already in the subject.

A synthetic statement is one in which the predicate is *not* contained in the subject. For example, "My computer is a Macintosh" is a synthetic statement. The predicate "is a Macintosh" adds information to the subject "My computer."

The strength of synthetic statements is that they tell us something new because the predicate is not contained in the subject. The weakness of synthetic statements is that they are not necessary — it is possible that I have made a mistake. Perhaps I am so ill informed about computers that I can't tell the difference between a Macintosh and an IBM computer that uses Microsoft Windows.

More Kinds of Sentences

We can combine the terms *a priori*, *a posteriori*, analytic, and synthetic in meaningful ways. For example:

- "All bachelors are male" is an analytic *a priori* statement. We know that this statement is true without having recourse to sensory knowledge, so therefore it is *a priori*. In addition, it is analytic because the predicate does not add information to the subject.

- "The grass is green" is a synthetic *a posteriori* statement. We know that this statement is true if we look outside and see that the grass is green (there has been no drought recently and snow does not cover the ground). Since we can check on the truth of this statement by using sensory information, it is *a posteriori*. In addition, it is synthetic because the predicate adds information not contained in the subject.

A kind of sentence that is impossible is an analytic *a posteriori* sentence. *A posteriori* statements are made after sense experience — that is, they are dependent on sense experience — but analytic statements are made independently of sense experience, so analytic *a posteriori* statements are impossible, being a contradiction in terms.

However, this leaves synthetic *a priori* statements. This kind of statement would be very useful to human beings, because this kind of statement would be certain, yet it would also contain new information. Kant believed that this kind of statement really exists.

According to Kant, the following sentence is an example of a synthetic *a priori* statement; that is, it is both necessary and informative:

- 7 + 5 = 12.

The synthetic *a priori* statement "7 + 5 = 12" may surprise you, as you may think that it is an analytic *a priori* statement. However, according to Kant, you can analyze "7 + 5" all you like, but you will never find "12." Since the predicate "= 12" is not contained in the subject "7 + 5," the sentence "7 + 5 = 12" is synthetic.

To say the same thing in other words: If "7 + 5 = 12" were to be analytic, the predicate "= 12" would have to be contained in the subject "7 + 5." But according to Kant, this is not the case, because all the subject "7 + 5" tells us is that the numbers 7 and 5 are being added together. The subject "7 + 5" does not tell us what the sum of these two numbers will be.

In addition, the statement "7 + 5 = 12" is also *a priori*. It is a necessary sentence that we know without having any sensory experience. After all, numbers don't exist in the physical universe. You may have seen five apples, but you have never seen a "five." The number "5" written on a chalkboard is only a symbol.

Furthermore, even if we take seven apples and five apples, put them together and count twelve apples, all that our sensory information would tell us is that these particular apples added together total twelve apples. It would not tell us that all groups containing seven apples and an additional five apples will total twelve apples.

Are you still unconvinced that the mathematical statement "12 + 5 = 12" is synthetic? Quick, analyze this subject — don't use a calculator! — "the square root of 123.456789" and then fill in the predicate of this sentence:

"The square root of 123.456789 equals ...."

Are you still convinced that mathematical statements of this kind are analytic?

Causality and the Categories of the Understanding

According to Kant, the sentence "Everything which happens has its cause" is a synthetic *a priori* sentence. This is something that we know prior to sensory experience and the predicate adds something that is not contained in the subject.

Therefore, according to Kant, causality is a synthetic *a priori* concept. It is one of Kant's twelve "categories of the understanding," in terms of which we must think about the world. In other words, our minds are made in such a way that we must think about the world in terms of causality and 11 other synthetic *a priori* concepts. One of these other synthetic *a priori* concepts is the concept of substance.

In Kant's analysis of human knowledge, both reason and the senses play a role. Knowledge begins with sensory experience; however, the mind contributes concepts in terms of which we must analyze that sensory experience. In other words, we must analyze our sensory experience of the world in terms of such concepts as cause and effect, and substance.

In doing so, we have no choice. Our minds are made in such a way that we *have* to experience the world in this way. It is possible that cause and effect, and substance, do not really exist. But if they don't, we will never be able to tell because we are prisoners of our own minds.

Conclusion

To conclude this essay, let me tell you about Peter Ustinov, a noted actor, director, teller of stories, writer, wit, etc. Someone once asked him why he read so many books. He replied that he did so because since he is a prisoner of his own mind, he wants it to be well furnished.

Note: The quotations by Kant that appear in this essay are from his *Critique of Pure Reason*, translated by Norman Kemp Smith.

SOCIAL AND POLITICAL PHILOSOPHY
Chapter 11: Thomas Hobbes (1588-1679): Leviathan

Thomas Hobbes (1588-1679) is a philosopher whose work has been important in political philosophy as well as in ethics. Hobbes believed that although Humankind is selfish by nature, it is able through reason and its selfish desires to create a government in which we can live in peace.

Psychological Egoism

First, however, we need to describe Hobbes' theory of human psychology. Hobbes was a Psychological Egoist. This means that Hobbes believed that everyone always acts selfishly; in other words, we always looks out for No. 1: ourselves. No matter what we do, we are acting selfishly, according to Hobbes.

The State of Nature

Hobbes' theory of Psychological Egoism allows us to investigate what would be in our own best self-interest. Should we always take what we want, whenever we want it? Is that in our own best self-interest? Or would it be better to live some other way?

Let's look at Hobbes' State of Nature — the way Humankind lived before a government was created. In the State of Nature, goods are scarce and there is competition for them. (Not everyone can own beachfront property and be the Chair of the Board of General Motors.) One reason for the competition is that by the Right of Nature everyone has the right to do whatever is necessary to preserve and enhance his or her life.

According to Hobbes, "The right of nature, which writers commonly call *jus naturale*, is the liberty each man hath to use his own power, as he will himself, for the preservation of his own nature; that is to say, of his own life; and consequently, of doing anything, which in his own judgment and reason, he shall conceive to be the aptest means thereunto." In other words, you have a right to everything you need to preserve and enhance your life.

One result of this is that people are so busy trying to protect what they have that they have no time to create new goods. If someone has many goods, they have to continually watch over and protect them because if they don't, someone will try to take the goods away from them.

Furthermore, in the State of Nature, everyone is roughly equal in the ability to kill. I would say that this is true today. If I have a gun, I can shoot Arnold Schwarzenegger and strong as he is, he won't be able to stop a bullet. Hobbes also believed that people are roughly equal in intelligence and other abilities.

Therefore, in the State of Nature, there is no justice or injustice, no right or wrong, because there is no room for them. Justice/injustice and right/wrong come into play only when we have a government to enforce laws. However, in the State of Nature, there is good and bad, but these terms are relative: What is good for me may be bad for you.

The State of Nature leads to war because of the desire and competition for scarce goods that cannot be shared. War comes about for three reasons, according to Hobbes: 1) competition for scarce goods, 2) diffidence (Hobbes used this word to mean a lack of trust and faith) — that is, fear that others may harm you if you don't harm them first, and 3) the desire for glory. In a famous quotation, Hobbes wrote that in the State of Nature "what is worst of all, [there is] continual fear, and danger of violent death; and the life of man [is] solitary, poor, nasty, brutish, and short."

Peace

However, Humankind has found a way out of the State of Nature, thanks to Humankind's selfish nature and the use of his reason. The State of Nature is a poor state to be in indeed. Because of the competition for scarce goods, you can't enjoy whatever you have because someone is always trying to take it from you. Therefore, we need Peace so that we can enjoy our life and whatever goods we have without worrying about other people trying to take them from us.

The Articles of Peace and the Commonwealth

We can achieve Peace by using the Articles of Peace and forming a Commonwealth ("a nation or state governed by the people; a republic" — *The American Heritage Dictionary*). There are several Articles of Peace, which are rules discovered by the use of our reason.

The first Article of Peace is "*that every man ought to endeavor peace, as far as he has hope of obtaining it; and when he cannot obtain it, that he may seek and use all helps and advantages of war.*" This first Article of Peace can be divided into two parts. The first part is "Seek peace and follow it." The second part is "Defend ourselves by all means possible."

Hobbes is saying here that everyone should endeavor to be at peace with his or her neighbors. When you are at peace, you are not planning to attack your neighbor, even if your neighbor has something that you desire. However, if peace is not available, then you can resort to war. Therefore, you let your neighbor enjoy his or her life in peace; however, if your neighbor should try to harm you, you are justified in trying to harm your neighbor.

The second Article of Peace is *"that a man be willing, when others are so too, as far forth as for peace and defense of himself he shall think it necessary, to lay down this right to all things; and be contented with so much liberty against other men, as he would allow other men against himself."* According to the Right of Nature, you have a right to everything — if someone else has something you desire, you have the right to take it from him or her. However, this leads to the State of Nature, in which other people are taking to take from you the things they desire. To get out of the State of Nature, you don't try to take from other people what they have — as long as they don't try to take from you what you have. It's important that you realize that you are not giving up your Right of Nature for all time, you are merely restraining it — as long as other people do the same thing. If they don't, then you may — if you choose — go to war.

The third Article of Peace is *"that men perform their covenants made."* We need an enforcer to make sure people keep their covenants (agreements); therefore, we need a government (commonwealth) to be this enforcer. One of the great inventions of Humankind is Law. Hobbes believed in a social contract theory of government. Human beings have an agreement with their government. In this agreement, all humans are supposed to obey the laws; if someone disobeys the laws, that person can be punished.

Everyone benefits from the formation of a just government with a system of laws and with police to make sure that everyone obeys the laws. Human beings are able to escape from the State of Nature. Instead of piling up goods, then having to worry constantly about people trying to take them from you, you will be able to relax a little more. Other people may not keep their agreement to restrain their right to everything and they may try to take your goods, but you have the power of the government behind you. It's the duty of the police to protect your goods and to capture and punish anyone who illegally tries to take your goods. Because people fear punishment, they are very likely to leave you and your goods alone.

There are many other Articles of Peace. One of the more interesting is "*that in revenges* [— that is, retribution of evil for evil —] *men look not at the greatness of the evil past, but the greatness of the good to follow.*" Apparently, Hobbes believed that punishment should be rehabilitative in nature.

Interestingly, Hobbes believes that all of the Articles of Peace can be summed up in one formulation of the Golden Rule: "*Do not that to another, which thou wouldst not have done to thyself.*"

Be sure that you understand this point: Hobbes believes that all of us always act selfishly; however, he believes that it is in our own best self-interest to form a government with a system of laws and with police to enforce the laws, and for us to obey the laws so that we can escape from the State of Nature.

Note: The quotations by Hobbes that appear in this essay are from his book *Leviathan*.

Chapter 12: John Locke (1632-1704): The State and the State of Nature

John Locke (1632-1704) is very important in social and political philosophy in part because of the influence he had upon the formation of the government of the United States. After all, Locke's ideas appear in the Declaration of Independence, the Constitution, and the Bill of Rights.

In *Concerning Civil Government*, Locke wrote about his ideas concerning the state of nature, property, the beginning of political societies, the ends (purposes) of political society, and when a government can legitimately be overthrown.

Of the State of Nature

The state of nature is the state in which Humankind is in before the formation of governments. It is possible that Humankind has always lived together in societies, so the state of nature may have never actually existed in history. However, it can be useful to think of a hypothetical state of nature in attempting to understand the basis on which political societies are formed.

Locke believed that the state of nature "is a state of perfect freedom." In it, people can "order their actions and dispose of their possessions and persons as they see fit ... without asking leave, or depending upon the will of any other man. According to Locke, in the state of nature, all men are "equal one amongst another."

In addition, everyone has a right of punishment in the state of nature. If someone commits a crime against you, then you have — in the state of nature — a right to punish that person. If someone steals something from you, you have the right to get the stolen item back, plus punish the thief so that he is less likely to steal again.

Of Property

One piece of property that everyone has a right to is their own body, which was created by God. In addition, Locke writes, "God, who hath given the world to men in common, hath also given them reason to make use of it to the best advantage of life and convenience. The earth and all that is therein is given to men for the support and comfort of their being."

This is very Biblical, of course, since in Genesis, Humankind is supposed to take care of the Garden of Eden. In addition, Locke believes very much in the right to private property. The earth is given to all in common; however, by dint of hard work, individual human beings can accumulate wealth. Locke believes that when we work with the earth, we are mixing our labor with it, and therefore we are entitled to the fruits of our labors.

For example, a forest in the wilderness may belong to all Humankind; however, a person who comes along and chops down some trees is entitled to sell the lumber and to start a farm on the cleared land.

According to Locke, "Though the earth and all inferior creatures be common to all men, yet every man has a property in his own person; this nobody has any right to but himself. The labor of his body and the work of his hands we may say are properly his. Whatsoever, then, he removes out of the state that nature hath provided and left it in, he hath mixed his labor with, and joined to it something that is his own, and thereby makes it his property."

Of the Beginning of Political Societies

In the state of nature, people are "by nature all free, equal, and independent." Political societies are brought into being only through the agreement with other people to form a political society. This, of course, is the social contract. People form a political society in order to have "a secure enjoyment of their properties, and a greater security against any [people] that are not part of it."

In the political society, the majority rules. It is the majority that determines what kind of government shall be allowed to exist, whether a democracy or a kingdom.

In Locke's words, "And thus every man, by consenting with others to make one body politic under one government, puts himself under an obligation to every one of that society, to submit to the determination of the majority, and to be concluded by it ...."

Also according to Locke, if you enjoy the fruits of living under a government, you are obligated to be obedient to the laws of that government. For by enjoying the fruits of the government, you are giving "tacit support" to that government. Thus, if you enjoy the police protection and the public libraries of the government, then you should pay your taxes.

Of the Ends of Political Society and Government

Of course, in the state of nature, Humankind is completely free, so why would people agree to join together and to give up some of their freedom? According to Locke, people agree to do this because they will benefit from doing it.

In Locke's words, "The great and chief end ... of men's uniting into commonwealths, and putting themselves under government, is the preservation of their property ...."

In the state of nature, three things are lacking that are conducive to the preservation of property:

1) In the state of nature, a set of established laws is lacking whereby people agree on what is right and wrong and on the way to settle controversies between people. We need laws to tell people what they can and cannot do.

2) In the state of nature, judges are lacking, who will justly and impartially settle controversies between people in accordance with the law. We need judges to settle cases in accordance with the law.

3) In the state of nature, power is lacking to back up punishments. We need a government that will have the power to give out a just punishment — the guilty will not go unpunished.

However, according to Locke, Humankind gives up two powers in order to form a political society:

1) The first power each person gives up is the power "to do whatsoever he thinks fit for the preservation of himself, and others within the permission of the law of nature, by which law, common to them all, he and all the rest of mankind are of one community, make up one society, distinct from all other creatures." You can't do just anything you want to preserve your life.

2) The second power Humankind gives up is the power "to punish the crimes committed against that law." When someone breaks the

law, the law courts must decide on the punishment. You can't kill someone because he stole your stereo.

Of the Dissolution of Government

Governments can be dissolved in many ways. One way is from without, as when a country is conquered by an invading army. Another way is from within; for example, when the legislative (legislature) is altered. When, say, someone begins to make laws who does not have the authority to make laws (perhaps someone is making laws who has not been voted into office), then "the people are at liberty to provide for themselves by erecting a new legislative, differing from the other, by the change of persons, or form, or both, as they shall find it most for their safety and good."

According to Locke, Humankind is justified in rebelling against a government when that government no longer protects the interests of the governed and when that government does not operate with their consent.

In Locke's words,

> Whensoever, therefore, the legislative shall [...] either by ambition, fear, folly, or corruption, endeavor to grasp themselves or put into the hands of any other an absolute power over the lives, liberties, and the estates of the people, by this breach of trust they forfeit the power the people had put into their hands, for quite contrary ends, and it devolves to the people, who have a right to resume their original natural liberty, and by the establishment of the new legislative (such as they shall think fit) provide for their own safety and security, which is the end for which they are in society.

Note: The quotations by Locke that appear in this essay are from his book *Concerning Civil Government [Second Treatise of Government]*.

Chapter 13: John Stuart Mill (1806-1873): The Case for Liberty and Law

John Stuart Mill is known for his work in such areas as morality, logic, the emancipation of women, and political science. In *On Liberty* (1859), he defends Humankind's freedom against the encroachments of governments.

I. Civil, or Social, Liberty

Mill's subject in *On Liberty* is civil, or social, liberty — that is, "the nature and limits of the power which can be legitimately exercised by society over the individual." As part of the background of this topic, he traces the history of struggles of the individual (for Liberty) against government (Authority). Liberty here means "protection against the tyranny of the political rulers."

In the early history of society, Humankind was much afraid of the power of governments, although this power was regarded as necessary. (Hobbes believed that the Commonwealth should have power to make sure everyone obeys the rules.) However, individuals were afraid of this power. To limit the power of the government, individuals wanted certain rights recognized and constitutional checks on the power of the government.

In recent history, however, the focus has changed. At one time kingships were hereditary. Now we are governed by politicians whom we can vote out of office. These representatives are supposed to identify themselves with the people and represent their interests.

The result, however, is a "tyranny of the majority." In a democracy, the groups of people who are most numerous rule over the rest because they have the most influence over the lawmakers, who, after all, are voted into office.

These lawmakers have two ways in which to go wrong:

1) They can issue mandates that require individuals to do wrong, and

2) They can issue mandates in areas where they ought not to interfere at all.

For example, lawmakers can raise taxes for an unjust war, thus forcing citizens to support evil. Or lawmakers can put into effect regulations that interfere in people's lives without just cause; for example, some people believe that two consenting adults ought to be able to have sex in their own home behind closed doors, even if they are homosexual. The writer Gore Vidal also believes that all drugs ought to be legal and that a woman ought to have the right to choose to have an abortion.

The next question that Mill considers is, Are one's feelings an adequate guide to making laws? This is something he rejects because people's feelings vary notoriously. If we are to reform society, it must be on a firmer foundation than that.

II. Mill's Principle and Beliefs

So on what foundation ought we to decide "the nature and limits of the power which can be legitimately exercised by society over the individual"? Mill has an answer: "[T]he sole end for which mankind are warranted, individually or collectively, in interfering with the liberty of action of any of their number, is self-protection." According to Mill, an adult has this right: "Over himself, over his own body and mind, the individual is sovereign."

This principle, however, does not apply to children. If a child wants to play in the street, we are justified in telling the child no. If a child does not want to go to school, we are justified in making the child go. This principle applies "only to human beings in the maturity of their faculties."

However, one should also be aware that there are some things a person cannot do. For example, I cannot harm another person. This means, of course, I cannot murder, I cannot rape, I cannot steal, I cannot beat up, etc.

In addition, a person may legitimately be forced to do some things. For example, I may be forced to give evidence in a court of law, I may be forced to defend my country during wartime, and I may be required to save someone's life (I cannot simply allow someone to die when I can easily save him or her).

Mill writes about what a free society — if it really is free — must have. A free society must have these three things:

1) [F]reedom in "the inward domain of consciousness"; "liberty of conscience"; "liberty of thought and feeling; absolute freedom of opinion and sentiment in all subjects, practical or speculative."

For example, I am entitled to my own opinion about evolution — I can either believe in it or not, as I choose. I am also entitled to my own opinion about whether the President of the United States is a good person or not.

2) "[L]iberty of tastes and pursuits; of framing the plan of our life to suit our own character; of doing as we like, subject to such consequences as may follow: without impediment from our fellow creatures, so long as what we do does not harm them, even though they think our conduct foolish, perverse, or wrong."

For example, if I want to join a commune and run naked through the woods, I can. If I want to be homeless, I can — as long as I don't harm other people.

3) "[C]ombination among individuals; freedom to unite, for any purpose not involving harm to others: the persons combining being supposed to be of full age, and not forced or deceived."

For example, if I want to join the American Nazi Party, I can — as long as I don't harm other people.

Majority opinion does not count here. According to Mill, "If all mankind minus one were of one opinion, and only one person were of the contrary opinion, mankind would be no more justified in silencing that one person, than he, if he had the power, would be justified in silencing mankind."

III. Two Objections

Mill's position is very clear. However, in addition to stating what he believes, he also responds to two objections that people could level against his thesis.

Objection #1. There should be no discussion in the case of a false belief.

Mill's response: "However unwillingly a person who has a strong opinion may admit the possibility that his opinion may be false, he ought to be moved by the consideration that, however true it may be, if it is not fully, frequently, and fearlessly discussed, it will be held as a dead dogma, not a living truth."

Even if you are absolutely sure that you are right, you need arguments supporting what you believe. Otherwise, when you finally come across someone who does not believe as you do, you will be unlikely to withstand his or her arguments.

Objection #2. We should allow free discussion only when the manner of arguing is temperate and fair.

Mill's response has four parts:

1. Any opinion that is silenced may, for all we know, be true.

2. Even if the opinion is in error, part of it may be true. The only way that we are able to improve our own opinions, and make them truer, is to subject them to criticism. We ought not to silence the critics for they perform a valuable function, even when they are wrong.

3. Let us suppose that the majority opinion is the whole truth. Unless it is debated, it is in danger of becoming merely a prejudice — with people not realizing the grounds for believing it. (Frequently, people become Republicans or Democrats simply because that is the way their parents voted.)

4. Unless an opinion is debated, people will pay only lip service to it. For people to truly believe it, it must be debated.

Let me add: If we are truly to understand our own opinion, we must understand the opinions of those opposed to us. In philosophy, we try to do this. We do our best to formulate arguments supporting our opinions, but we also listen to the arguments supporting the other opinions. Only in this way can the truth be known.

IV. Two Maxims

As kind of a summary of his main points, Mill states these two maxims:

1. "[T]he individual is not accountable to society for his actions, in so far as these concern the interests of no person but himself."

2. "[T]hat for such actions as are prejudicial to the interests of others, the individual is accountable, and may be subjected either to social or to legal punishment, if society is of opinion that the one or the other is requisite for its protection."

V. Objections to Governmental Inference When Infringement of Liberty is Not an Issue

Finally, Mill considers objections to governmental inference when infringement of liberty is not an issue. According to Mill, we ought not to give the government power to do something when:

1. The thing to be done is likely to be better done by individuals than by the government.

2. Though individuals may not do the thing so well as the government, it may be desirable that it be done nevertheless by individuals.

3. Adding unnecessarily to the power of the government may be a great evil.

VI. Conclusion

Mill's essay is titled *On Liberty* for a reason: he believes in the liberty of the individual to think for him- or herself. This right is unqualified.

Chapter 14: Kai Nielsen (1925-2021): In Defense of Egalitarianism

The glossary of the textbook *Fundamentals of Philosophy*, by David Stewart and H. Gene Blocker, defines "egalitarian" as the "[p]olitical doctrine that no one has a right to a greater share of social goods [defined by Stewart and Blocker as 'money, power, respect, education, health care, and so on'] than another; that individuals do not deserve the results of superior innate talents and abilities."

In opposition to egalitarian is libertarian, which Stewart and Blocker define as the "[p]olitical doctrine that each individual should be maximally free from governmental restraint, especially as regards the freedom of the individual to accumulate and dispose of an unequal share of social goods through superior intelligence, or other talents and abilities."

The classic advocate of egalitarianism is Karl Marx, the father of Communism; however, a contemporary exponent of egalitarianism is the philosopher Kai Nielsen (born 1925). Nielsen defended egalitarianism in his 1985 book, *Equality and Liberty: A Defense of Radical Egalitarianism* (published by Rowman and Littlefield).

Equality and Egalitarianism

Nielsen begins by attempting to make clear the notions of equality and egalitarianism. These notions currently are unclear. After all, many people who are against egalitarianism will say that they are for certain rights for everyone (for example, the rights that are protected by the Bill of Rights).

In addition, many people who are against egalitarianism will say that they are for moral equality; that is, as Nielsen writes, "Persons must all be treated as moral persons of equal worth; in this way they must all be treated as equals." However, these people who are against egalitarianism go on to say that we must not treat people "identically." Nielsen agrees with this: "A child and a very old and ill person should not be treated the same. But no egalitarian thinks that they should."

There are some things that once defined egalitarianism but which are now accepted by conservatives, such as "equal legal and political rights for all members of a society." However, Nielsen points out that although such rights are guaranteed by a society, say in a constitution, despite such "formal legal and political equality," in reality there can be "substantive inequalities in legal protection and political power."

For example, by law I can run for President of the United States; however, because I lack the necessary political contacts and sufficient funds to run for high office, I am unable to mount a credible campaign. Another example: A person who is on trial can often get a better defense if he or she can pay for a battery of expensive, high-powered attorneys than if he or she has to rely on a court-appointed attorney (often new to the legal profession). Therefore, according to egalitarians, if we are ever to achieve legal, political, and social equalities, we must also achieve economic equality.

Equality as a Goal or Ideal, and as a Right

It is possible to look at equality as a goal or ideal, or as a right. First Nielsen looks at economic equality as a goal:

> As a goal, as an ideal state of affairs to be obtained, an egalitarian is committed to trying to provide the social basis for an equality of *condition* for all human beings. The ideal, putting it minimally as a first step, is to provide the social basis for an equality of life prospects such that there cannot be anything like the vast disparities in whole life prospects that exist now.

Nielsen finds it simply unfair that two children who have equal intelligence and equal abilities should have different life prospects because of who their parents are. The child of a successful businessperson can look forward to college, law school, travel in Europe, etc., while the child of a person getting public assistance can look forward only to inadequate food, shelter, clothing, and education. Both children may have the formal right of attending Harvard if they get accepted, but in reality, only one of the children (despite their being of equal intelligence) has the real-life possibility of attending Harvard.

To Nielsen, egalitarianism has as a goal the elimination of having such different life prospects simply as a result of which social class you are born into. To do this, however, we need an equality of wealth. As Nielsen writes, "It is as evident as anything can be that there is a close correlation between wealth and power."

However, Nielsen also argues that "a certain kind of equality is a right." He describes first the egalitarian goal: "That everyone, where this is reasonably possible, is to have his or her needs equally met is an egalitarian *goal*." In addition to this goal are the egalitarian rights: "that people be treated as equals, that in the design of our institutions people have an equal right to respect, that none be treated as a means only, are natural *rights*." (Natural rights are those rights "which need not be legal rights or rights which must be conventionally acknowledged.")

Conservatives and Social Justice

Conservatives totally reject "an equality of condition." They don't want to see an equality of outcome, where, for example, a physician who has struggled through a dozen years of higher education makes the same income as a fast food worker who dropped out of high school. Conservatives would say that the physician deserves a higher income because he or she worked harder than the fast food worker.

Nielsen, however, writes, "Liberal egalitarians ... are wary of appealing to the concept of desert. Our social and natural inheritance — that is, what kind of people we are and what our abilities and opportunities are — are in important ways beyond our control and are subject to all sorts of contingencies for which we are not, and indeed cannot be, responsible."

For example, suppose that the physician has a very high IQ, while the fast food worker has a very low IQ. Both people are using their IQ and are not wasting their intelligence. In addition, both people were born with their respective IQs — this is not something that anyone has control over. (Environment can raise or lower one's IQ a little, but basically you are born with a certain IQ.)

In addition, the skills that you were born with may or may not be useful in today's society. If you were born with the potential to acquire computer-programming skills (which require abstract thinking), then you can train yourself for a job that is in demand. However, if you were born with the potential to be a great mountain man, then your potential skills are not in much demand — you should have been born a couple of centuries earlier, when the American West was being opened. Obviously, we do not control which century we are born in.

Conceptions of Radical Egalitarian Justice

There are a number of conceptions of radical egalitarian justice; however, Nielsen writes, they share an emphasis "on attaining, in attaining social justice, some central equality of condition for everyone. Some egalitarians stress some prized condition such as self-respect or a good life; others, more mundanely, but at least as crucially, stress an overall equal sharing of the various good things and bad things of the society."

Two Principles of Egalitarian Justice

Nielsen has two principles of egalitarian justice:

> 1) "Each person is to have an equal right to the most extensive total system of equal basic liberties and opportunities (including equal opportunities for meaningful work, for self-determination and political and economic participation) compatible with a similar treatment of all. (This principle gives expression to a commitment to attain and/or sustain equal moral autonomy and equal self-respect.)"

This means that everyone will have an equal right to such social goods as food, shelter, clothing, education, health care, and so on.

> 2) "After provisions are made for common social (community) values, for capital overhead to preserve the society's productive capacity, allowances made for differing unmanipulated [for example, not manipulated by Madison Avenue] needs and preferences, and due weight is given to the just entitlements of individuals, the income and wealth (the common stock of means) is to be so divided that each person will have an equal right to an equal share."

Nielsen's second principle of egalitarian justice does not mean that all wealth will be divided equally. Part of the product of a society will be used for public goods (roads, hospitals, schools, public libraries). Part will be used "to protect future generations" (a clean environment). Part will be used to "preserve the society's productive capacity" (to build and maintain factories, etc.).

What is left of the social product will be used to meet people's needs "as fully as possible" and "as equally as possible." This does not mean that everyone will be treated equally. For example, a child who wants skates will be given skates, and a child who wants snowshoes will be given snowshoes. (It's easy to tell that Nielsen taught in Canada.)

Nielsen's Tool for Attaining Equality

Nielsen intends for his second principle of egalitarian justice to be a tool — "a tool in trying to attain a state of affairs where there are no considerable differences in life prospects between different groups of people because some have a far greater income, power, authority or privilege than others."

Justice

Nielsen believes that justice demands that people, if possible, be given equal shares. But what if it is impossible to give equal shares? For example, life-saving medical resources may be so scarce that there are not enough to go around. Nielsen gives three examples and tells which recommendations he thinks would be consistent with egalitarian justice.

In each of the three examples, two people need blood for a transfusion, but there is not enough blood for both of them. In the first example, two people, person A and person B, need the blood. Both persons are similar, but person A has frequently donated blood, while person B has not. Many people would say that A should be given the blood, and Nielsen does not disagree, despite being hesitant to say that person A deserves the blood.

In the second example, two people are similar in many ways, but person A′ is a young woman with three children, and would be healthy after the transfusion. Person B′ is a 90-year-old woman with a feeble intellect, who will probably die soon even after receiving the transfusion. Nielsen would give the blood to the young woman because that way, more needs — those of the young woman's children — would be satisfied.

In the final example, person A′′ is a community's only doctor, while person B′′ is the town drunk. Nielsen would give the blood to the doctor because of social utility ("the overall good of the community").

According to Nielsen, the important thing in the three cases is that giving the blood to person A, person A′, and person A′′ does not violate his second principle of egalitarian justice. All the people's interests — those of A, A′, A′′, B, B′, and B′′ — are being considered equally.

As Nielsen writes, "We start from a baseline of equality. If there were none of these differences between them, if there were no other relevant differences, there would be no grounds to choose between them. We could not, from a moral point of view, simply favor A because he was A. Just as human beings, as moral persons or persons who can become capable of moral agency, we do not distinguish between them and we must treat them equally."

Note: The quotations by Kai Nielsen that appear in this essay are from his book *Equality and Liberty: A Defense of Radical Egalitarianism.*

Chapter 15: John Rawls (1921-2002): A Theory of Justice

Distributive justice is concerned with the distribution of goods in a society. For example, how much of a safety net should there be for the poor? Should people be allowed to become as rich as their talents and luck can make them, even if it means other people must do without some kinds of goods because the rich have stockpiled them? Should every qualified person be given the opportunity to have a college education?

John Rawls (1921-2002), who was a professor at Harvard, is famous for his book *A Theory of Justice*, which was published in 1971. Rawls, I am sure, is a philosopher whose ideas will be studied a hundred years from now.

The Primary Problem of Justice

The primary problem of justice is deciding on principles that, if followed, will lead to a just society.

Obviously, we are affected by society throughout our lives, and therefore we hope that the society we live in is just. To have a just society, what Rawls calls "primary goods" must be distributed fairly. Primary goods include such things as basic rights and liberties and opportunities.

For example, wealth is a primary good because it is useful no matter what rational plan you have formed for your life. If you wish to have a career as a physician, wealth will help you pay for medical school. If you wish to raise a family, wealth will help you pay for the cost of food, shelter, and clothing for your spouse and children. A just society must distribute wealth fairly.

A Contractarian Perspective

As a social theorist, Rawls is a believer in the social contract theory. According to this theory, society is a contract between the state and its citizens. Both society and citizens have duties to each other; for example, the philosopher Thomas Hobbes believed that the citizens have a duty to obey the laws, and the state has a duty to ensure that covenants are kept.

Rawls does not believe that it is a historical fact that people sat down and decided to form a government. He writes that the social contract is to be "understood as a purely hypothetical situation characterized so as to lead to a certain conception of justice."

In deciding upon the rules for a just society, Rawls suggests that people ought to deliberate under a veil of ignorance; that is, people will not know in advance what position they will have in that society.

Therefore, in the original position (the position one is in before a society has been formed and before one knows one's position in it), one will not know one's economic status, one's race, one's creed, one's intelligence, one's career, etc.

Because of this, Rawls believes that people will form just rules. For example, if you don't know in advance what race you will be, you won't form Jim Crow rules because you may end up being the race that is discriminated against. If you don't know in advance whether you will be poor or wealthy, you won't make rules that favor the rich over the poor because you may be poor.

Rawls also believes that rational people will choose to obey the maximin rule, which states that we will choose the best of the worst situations (the "best-worse" outcome). In other words, we will choose a society that makes things as good as possible for the least advantaged citizens; after all, since we are behind a veil of ignorance, we don't know that we won't be among the least advantaged citizens: poor, with a low IQ and few skills, etc.

Two Principles of Justice

To ensure the fair distribution of society's primary goods, Rawls argues for two basic principles of justice. The first principle is the Principle of "Equal Basic Liberty for All." Rawls states the principle in this way:

> Each person is to have an equal right to the most extensive total system of equal basic liberties compatible with a similar system of liberty for all.

This principle means that everyone will have certain rights to basic liberties. These basic liberties are guaranteed in the United States by the Bill of Rights; Rawls writes that these basic liberties include:

> (a) freedom to participate in the political process (the right to vote, the right to run for office, etc.)

> (b) freedom of speech (including freedom of the press)

> (c) freedom of conscience (including religious freedom)

(d) freedom of the person (as defined by the concept of the rule of law)

(e) freedom from arbitrary arrest and seizure, and

(f) the right to hold personal property.

The second principle is the Difference Principle. Rawls states the principle in this way:

Social and economic inequalities are to be arranged so that they are both: (a) to the greatest benefit of the least advantaged, ... and (b) attached to offices and positions open to all under conditions of fair equality of opportunity.

As you can see above, the Difference Principle consists of two parts. The first part states that some differences in society will be allowed, but only if these differences are to the advantage of the least advantaged in society.

For example, one difference that we may allow in society is that physicians can make more money than those whose careers do not require years of preparation in medical school and internships. We will allow physicians to make more money than other workers because if we don't, we would have fewer physicians than we need. Of course, having enough physicians is to the advantage of the least advantaged in society.

The second part of the Difference Principle states that these positions of social and economic inequalities must be open to all — that all must have an equal opportunity to fill these positions. Thus, if a person with rich parents and a person with poor parents are equally qualified and desire to become physicians, we must allow the person with poor parents an opportunity to become a physician, perhaps through the government subsidizing his or her medical school costs.

Rawls sums up the Difference Principle in this way:

While the distribution of wealth and income need not be equal, it must be to everyone's advantage, and at the same time, positions of authority and offices of command must be accessible to all. One applies the second principle by holding positions open, and then, subject to this constraint, arranges social and economic inequalities so that everyone benefits.

According to Rawls, these "two principles ... are a special case of a more general conception of justice that can be expressed in this way:

> All social values — liberty and opportunity, income and wealth, and the bases of self-respect — are to be distributed equally unless an unequal distribution of any, or all, of these values is to everyone's advantage.

Lexical Priority

Since we have two principles, we need to decide what to do in the cases in which the principles conflict and so we cannot satisfy both principles. To make decisions in these cases we need to ecide which principle is most important and so must be satisfied before the other principle can be satisfied. Fortunately, Rawls tells us which principle has what he calls "lexical priority," meaning that it must be satisfied before the other principle may legitimately be satisfied.

The principle that has greatest lexical priority is the Principle of "Equal Basic Liberty for All." Rawls believes that we have certain rights that cannot be taken away from us even if restricting them will bring all of us even more material goods.

For example, society cannot take away our free speech even if it means each of us will have more material goods. (The People's Republic of China managed to stop mass starvation, but it also severely restricted the rights of its people. Rawls would regard the Chinese society as unjust.)

However, society can restrict our rights if doing so will provide more liberty to everyone. For example, we have the right to free speech, including freedom of the press. However, we can restrict the press' right to report on a trial if restricting that right will result in a fair trial. (Sometimes, unrestricted freedom of the press can result in biased trials.)

To recap: The principle that has lexical priority is the Principle of "Equal Basic Liberty for All." This means that our basic liberties cannot be traded away, as they might be if we used a utilitarian position. For example, during the slavery days of the United States, some utilitarians defended slavery by saying that it was necessary for the economic development of the South. Therefore, in return for economic advantages, white southerners traded away the basic rights of African-Americans. Rawls' theory would not permit this.

Rawls Presents a Compromise

There are two competing opposite theories about distributive justice. The egalitarian theory argues for equality in all areas. However, Rawls' theory allows for differences, provided the two subprinciples in the Difference Principle are met (and providing that the Principle of "Equal Basic Liberty for All" is met). The libertarian theory argues for complete freedom in the marketplace. However, Rawls' theory does not allow for our basic rights and liberties to be traded away. Therefore, Rawls' theory presents a compromise between egalitarianism and libertarianism.

Note: The quotations by John Rawls that appear in this essay are from his book *A Theory of Justice*.

Chapter 16: Fighting McCarthyism: Ohio University Prof, Supreme Court, Defeat Loyalty Oath

By David Bruce

Published 11 December 1989 in *The Athens News* (Ohio).

In 1950, Joe McCarthy, the junior senator from Wisconsin made a speech in Wheeling, West Virginia, that made him nationally prominent.

"Ladies and gentlemen, while I cannot take the time to name all the men in the State Department who have been named as active members of the Communist Party and members of a spy ring, I have here in my hand a list of 205—a list of names that were made known to the Secretary of State as being members of the Communist Party and who nevertheless are still working and shaping policy in the State Department."

Following that speech came years—the early to mid-1950s—in which McCarthy cast aspersions—with little or no evidence—about men and women innocent of any wrongdoing. McCarthy nearly immobilized two presidents, and because of his fame and the fear in which he cast the country, few dared to oppose him.

Ohio University Philosophy Professor Robert Wieman was exposed to much of that anti-communist hysteria in the early 1950s when he taught at Oklahoma A & M College. In a 1989 interview with *The Athens NEWS*, Wieman, who has taught at OU since the mid-'50s, told how in 1951, the Oklahoma legislature passed an anti-communist law, requiring all local and state employees to take a loyalty oath. The oath swore that the individual 1) was loyal to the United States, 2) was not a Communist, and 3) would bear arms, if necessary, in case of attack upon the United States.

Feeling that the law as drafted was unconstitutional, Wieman (a Navy veteran from 1942-46 who served much of the time in waters off Africa) and six other state employees at Oklahoma A & M went to court to force a test of the law's constitutionality. Eventually, the case which became known as Wieman vs. Updegraff, reached the U.S. Supreme Court.

But first, the case went before Oklahoma District Judge W.A. Carlisle, who rebuked the seven Oklahoma A & M employees:

"The people of the United States today are facing a terrible danger. We've reached the point where we must separate the wheat from the chaff. These people want all the other protections of the government but they say they wouldn't fight to defend this country if necessary. I say it's a travesty of justice. It's an outrage for people like that to draw public funds. If Washington were alive today, I wonder what he'd say about something like this. In my opinion, a man that wouldn't defend his country if necessary has no right to draw its money."

Carlisle ordered that the employees be fired and their pay withheld. Eventually, though, the Supreme Court ruled in favor of Wieman and the other state employees. The front-page headline in *The New York Times* read, "Oklahoma's Oath of Loyalty Killed."

In the Supreme Court decision, issued Dec. 15, 1952, Justice Hugo Black wrote:

"The Oklahoma statute is but one manifestation of a national network of laws aimed at coercing and controlling the minds of men. Test oaths are notorious tools of tyranny. When used to shackle the mind they are, or at least they should be, unspeakably odious to a people. Governments need and have ample power to punish treasonable acts. But it does not follow that they must have power to punish thought and speech as distinguished from acts."

This case had two important ramifications, Wieman pointed out. First, he said, there was an "emphatic reaffirmation of the legal system." According to Wieman, "McCarthyism is almost any passionately fanatic movement. Whether the people are always sincere in using it or are using it as a vehicle to win elections doesn't matter." In a movement that is passionate and fanatic and perhaps even sincere, he pointed out, there is a tendency to "say that procedure doesn't matter, only the end matters."

During the McCarthy era, Wieman recalled, many people were "hesitant to defend the procedural safeguards for the modification of policy and the bringing of consensus among people." His case allowed the U.S. Supreme Court and later the Oklahoma Supreme Court to offer their prestige and eloquent statements about why these procedural safeguards are important, the OU professor said. The case reaffirmed that the American system of laws is a procedural system which should not be sacrificed for a passionate commitment to some end which fanatics believe outweighs other people's rights, he said.

In addition, Wieman maintained, accommodation—finding a way in which people can live together with the least mutual obstruction and the most mutual contribution—is one way for people and nations to live among one another. The Supreme Court case led to more accommodation, while it generated more opposition to McCarthyism.

Before that, however, through smear campaigns and negative campaigns, McCarthy won elections, "If you can win elections by this kind of thing, it becomes a feeding frenzy," Wieman said. "It's hard for people to express themselves effectively if [their opinion] isn't swimming with that tide."

Today [December 1989] Wieman sees a return of some of the characteristics of McCarthyism. Professionals are acknowledging that elections are won these days by politicians and their advisers doing whatever it takes to win, fair or foul.

This Wieman calls an "extremism in relation to the past." Until recently, he said, "although running for re-election was a major concern of people in office, they didn't spend all their term running for their next election.

"Most people, unless they were desperately out and unlikely to win without some wild extremism, were unlikely to commit themselves to things, in order to win an election, that would then interfere with their being able to meet the problems of the nation once in office," he said.

Today, Wieman said, there is a "curious combination of cynicism with a quite sincere factional suspicion of people who hold views different from what we do." For example, he pointed out, for the most part anti-abortion and abortion rights advocates are not seeking an accommodation with one another. It is much the same with other major issues, he said.

Also, in politics today there is the belief that any proposal, to meet a crisis, that costs money is not politically practical. "And so," Wieman said, "we have the oddity of national governors who will discuss needs and discuss possible solutions to those needs and will declare in favor of those solutions to those needs, but then assume that somebody else will have to fund it—state or local governments."

"Well, if you decide that someone else is going to do something and pay for it, that's not the way things are going to get done," he said. "They get done by the people who are going to pay for them deciding that's what should be done."

After a candidate is elected, the professor noted, he or she doesn't face the needs of the nation; instead the candidate thinks about "what did I say I was going to do and how can I squirm out of it if at all.

"It paralyzes government," just as McCarthyism paralyzed government in the early '50s, Wieman said.

When you have a win-at-any-costs political mentality, "courage [becomes] a terribly expensive thing to have," Wieman said. "You don't win by being courageous, you win by attacking from the outside; and if you are in, by being defensive, by rhetoric.

"Do anything and you make some enemies somewhere," he continued. "You can't do anything without influencing some people more favorably and other people less favorably, and so they're not going to regard you as their best friends anymore." Because of this, some politicians conclude that they ought not to do anything, he lamented.

A philosopher, Wieman explained that "in philosophy, we think we're engaged in inquiry, working out a commitment to the underlying principles of inquiry and the intellectual life." And so the philosopher doesn't regard teaching at a university as a job, in which the employee must leave all important decisions to higher-ups. After all, according to Wieman, "Universities are made up of people like philosophers; they're not made up by the chairman of the board of regents who hires somebody to stand in front of the class."

****

Robert Wieman (1920-2002)
    https://www.findagrave.com/memorial/123156906/robert-m-wieman

****

Now retired, David Bruce taughe English and Philosophy at OU, and he wrote over 1,000 Wise Up! Anecdotes columns for The Athens News.

AESTHETICS

Chapter 17: H. Gene Blocker (born 1937): The Esthetic Attitude

A current controversy in esthetics is about whether there is such a thing as an esthetic attitude. The older traditional estheticians were Modernist in outlook, and believed that there was, but today these estheticians' theories are being challenged by the Postmodernist estheticians. In his essay, H. Gene Blocker (born 1937) explores this controversy, looking first at the ideas of Modernist estheticians and then at the ideas of Postmodernist estheticians. In addition, he shows how each group of critics feels about censorship of the arts.

The main assumption of the Modernist estheticians is that people can be interested in an art object — or other object — for different reasons. These reasons will determine the person's point of view and how he or she sees the object.

For example, a person could look at a forest for many different reasons. A logger may look at the forest in terms of how much lumber could be made from harvesting the timber. The owner of the forest could look at the forest in terms of money and wonder how much money could be made from harvesting the timber. An environmentalist could look at the forest as a habitat for wildlife. A family on an outing could look at the forest as a nice place for a short hike and a picnic lunch. A painter could look at the forest as a suitable subject for a landscape. A songwriter such as John Denver could be inspired by the forest to write a song about saving the environment. The different reasons people have for being interested in the forest influence the way they see the forest.

People have various attitudes when looking at the forest, and some of these attitudes can be grouped into the esthetic point of view. This, of course, brings up the question, "What is the esthetic point of view?" The Modernist answer of the older traditional estheticians is that the esthetic attitude is characterized by three things: disinterestedness, detachment, and emotional distance. To look at something esthetically, we look at it for its own sake; we cannot be distracted by thoughts of monetary gain or any other selfish calculations.

When we look at something for its own sake, we are saying that it has intrinsic value: It is valuable in itself, and not for anything that we can get out of it. To look at a forest solely in terms of the money to be gotten from logging is not to look at the forest as having any intrinsic value; instead, the forest is valued only for the money it can bring to the owner. In the case of nature songwriter John Denver, he can look at the forest as having intrinsic value, even if later he does write a best-selling song about the forest.

All of us regard esthetic experiences as possessing intrinsic value. As such, this kind of experience is unusual. Most of the time, we do not experience things esthetically. We merely look at something, but we do not see it esthetically. For example, I am a heavy coffee drinker, but I seldom take a close look at my coffee cup. Most mornings, I merely grab my empty coffee cup and fill it with coffee. (I'm groggy and unable to function well until I've had my first 20 cups of the morning. Joke.) But it is possible for me to look at my coffee cup esthetically: It has an esthetically pleasing shape, and on it is printed an esthetically pleasing picture of a hot air balloon floating above a beach.

However, some places encourage people to adopt an esthetic attitude. For example, at an art museum you are encouraged to look at art works. The lighting is focused on the art works so you can see them better, and you are not allowed to shout or engage in loud conversation; in fact, everything in the art museum encourages you to look at but not to interact with (don't touch the paintings, please!) the art works.

One result of the detachment of the esthetic attitude is that the art work is placed in isolation. The art work is regarded as a self-contained whole and is not directly connected to the rest of the world. For example, at the end of Shakespeare's *Hamlet*, the theater is strewn with "corpses," yet a few minutes later the actors playing the corpses will stand up, then bow to your applause. In the theater — which just like the art museum encourages the esthetic attitude — the audience knows that it is looking at fiction and not at real life. However, the audience engages in a "willing suspension of disbelief" and feels an emotional reaction when Hamlet dies. French philosopher Jean-Paul Sartre calls this the "unrealizing" function of esthetic experience.

Because the viewer of the art work is both disinterested and detached, he or she is reflective and contemplative and tends to look at the art work "symbolically." It is possible to look at a forest in terms of utilitarian considerations — for example, looking only at the money that can be made from cutting down the forest to make lumber. However, one can also look at the forest symbolically; in the forest we see the cycle of nature as trees grow from seeds, mature, then age and die. In addition, we can see how living creatures are related, as birds make their nests in the limbs of the tree and as the leaves that fall from the tree fertilize the earth for other vegetation.

In looking at the forest symbolically, Blocker writes, we see the "paradox of the esthetic attitude." The forest is something that is concrete, yet it can represent something that is abstract, such as rebirth and renewal — as when a forest grows back in an area where there has been a forest fire.

Blocker also writes that there can be an intense emotional interest in an object of esthetic attention at a symbolic level. For example, no one believes in worshipping the god Dionysus anymore. However, we can still enjoy such plays as Euripides' *Bacchae* today. (Bacchus is the Roman name of the Greek god Dionysus.) Why? Because of the symbolic level of the play. We look at Dionysus as representing the nonrational forces — the desire for fun and for play — inside us. Euripides' play shows that these forces must be recognized, for if they are bottled up, they can destroy you.

So far, Blocker has looked at the older traditional estheticians' theory of esthetic attitude in terms of disinterestedness, detachment, and emotional distance. Now he shows the relationship of this Modernist theory to the current controversy about censorship in the arts.

Today, many people, including many Postmodernist estheticians, would like to see the arts censored because they think that the way women are portrayed in the arts leads to violence against women. For example, they feel that art works of nude women encourage looking at women as mere objects.

Blocker points out two problems with this attitude:

1) We can ask whether portrayals of nude women really are likely to lead to violence against women. If the older traditional estheticians' theory of esthetic attitude in terms of disinterestedness, detachment, and emotional distance is correct, the answer is, no.

2) Women do symbolize certain qualities in art. Blocker writes, "Many art works represent women as symbols of fertility, emotion,

intuition, nurturing, passivity, weakness." These qualities may be stereotypes, but nevertheless women continue to be regarded as symbolizing them.

According to the Modernist estheticians, does looking at a painting of a female nude cause sexual desire or arousal? The answer is, no. The esthetic attitude is one of distance, and therefore one merely contemplates the art work. According to the Modernist estheticians, the art work will have only a temporary effect on the viewer — almost always, immediately after seeing an art work, the audience will continue to live the same way and have the same attitudes it did before.

However, according to the Postmodernist estheticians, there is no such thing as an esthetic attitude, and therefore the audience does not distance itself from the art work.

Also according to the Modernist estheticians, the audience is capable of temporarily assuming different attitudes. We can imagine holding different perspectives, without adopting them permanently. Thus, in a play a character may be a Marxist and spout Marxist ideas, yet the audience will hear the ideas, understand the Marxist character's perspective, but not become Marxists. As Blocker writes, "[M]ost of us can entertain but finally *resist* many different perspectives."

However, the Postmodernist estheticians who advocate censorship believe that we are not capable of temporarily holding attitudes. They believe that we are influenced by the ideas we come in contact with. They believe that viewing a sexist art work can make us into sexists.

There is no doubt that we are influenced by the ideas of our culture. The Modernist estheticians believe that popular culture influences us much more than fine arts. After all, we live in a consumer society and are constantly barraged by advertisements. A USAmerican adult who can go through an entire day without spending any money is unusual.

However, the Postmodernist estheticians deny that there is a valid distinction between popular culture and fine arts. We are influenced by all the ideas we come in contact with. Fine art and popular culture are merely different forms of the general culture, and both influence us. According to many Postmodernist estheticians, it is society that determines our values and attitudes. However, according to the Modernist estheticians, we are in control. The Modernist estheticians believe that we can try to understand the ideas of the artist without permanently adopting those ideas, but the Postmodernist estheticians believe that we will be influenced by those ideas whether we want to be influenced or not.

Because the Modernist estheticians believe that we are in control, they resist censorship. Because the Postmodernist estheticians believe that we are not in control, they advocate censorship.

Note: The quotations by Blocker that appear in this essay are from his essay "The Esthetic Attitude."

Chapter 18: Sir Kenneth Clark (1903-1983): The Naked and the Nude

The first chapter of *The Nude: A Study in Ideal Form* by Sir Kenneth Clark (1903-1983) is titled "The Naked and the Nude." In it, he draws a distinction between the naked and the nude. The naked is the human being without clothes. Imagine a dream in which you suddenly find yourself without any clothes in a group of fully clothed people. You will feel embarrassed. This is an example of the naked.

The nude, however, is depicted in art. The artist depicts an ideal form instead of the imperfect bodies that we are born with — or that we acquire through aging and bad habits. As such, the nude is an art form that was invented by a particular people — the Greeks — at a particular time — the fifth century B.C.E. Therefore, Sir Kenneth writes, "... the nude is not the subject of art, but a form of art."

Often, people believe that the naked human body is something that we are glad to see and are "glad to see depicted." But this is not the case. A nudist camp is filled with naked people, but this is hardly erotic, as many of the naked people will have bodies that are far from ideal. After all, an obese person can be a nudist, as a quick look through some nudist magazines will show you. Also, remember showering after high school gym class? Some of the bodies in the shower were far from ideal!

The naked human body is different from a landscape or an animal. Often, the artist can directly depict — without making changes to improve the subject — a landscape or an animal and thereby create a work of art. But a naked human being is unlikely to strike us as a work of art. As Sir Kenneth points out, even a photographer who photographs a naked human being is in search of the ideal of what a human body should be — but this ideal is difficult to find.

Because of this, Sir Kenneth writes, the naked human body is no more than a "point of departure for a work of art." However, the human body does have certain associations that are not lost in the work of art. For example, there is an eroticism in the naked human being. Human beings — like all creatures — wish to reproduce. Although some critics have denied that there is eroticism in art, Sir Kenneth points out that eroticism is obviously present in the nude.

Other aspects of human experience captured by the naked body, Sir Kenneth writes, include "harmony, energy, ecstasy, humility, pathos." Because of this, we may think that "the nude as a means of expression is of universal and eternal value," but Sir Kenneth states that this view is mistaken. The nude has been at home "[o]nly in countries touching on the Mediterranean."

Both Sir Kenneth and the ancient Greek philosopher Aristotle believe that in our search for physical beauty our instinctive desire is to perfect, not to imitate. The artist who creates a nude is in search of ideal beauty. Therefore, the chief assumption that underlies Sir Kenneth's and Aristotle's view is that ideal beauty exists. Readers will remember that among Plato's Forms or Ideas is Beauty.

Historically, when the artist tries to create ideal beauty, there have been two critical interpretations — neither of which Sir Kenneth finds satisfactory — of the ideal:

1) To achieve an ideal whole, the artist may take ideal parts from imperfect wholes and put them together. Thus, to create an ideal feminine nude, the artist may use one model for the face, another model for the arms, another model for the legs, another model for the breasts, etc.

Sir Kenneth rejects this interpretation because experience shows that such parts do not recombine well. A leg that seemed perfect when attached to an imperfect body will not seem perfect when attached to other parts that seemed perfect when they were attached to imperfect bodies.

2) To achieve an ideal whole, the artist may search for "the middle form." According to this idea, the beautiful is the average. The USAmerican actor Robert Redford is handsome because the distance between his eyes is average — if the distance were greater than average or shorter than average, he would not be handsome. All of Robert Redford's features are average — his nose is not too big or too small — and thus he is handsome.

Sir Kenneth rejects this interpretation because, he writes, "Beauty is precious and rare, and if it were like a mechanical toy, made up of parts of average size that could be put together at will, we should not value it as we do."

Nonetheless, Sir Kenneth states, proper proportion does play a role in beauty. The Greeks, who invented the nude, had some peculiarities of mind that led them to furnish the Western world with a pattern of perfection of the human form. For one thing, the Greeks had a "passion for mathematics." One of the most famous images of Renaissance art is the Italian Leonardo da Vinci's drawing of the man "squaring the circle." In doing so, Leonardo was influenced by Vitruvius, a Roman architect and writer who was active between 46 and 30 B.C.E. (Of course, the Romans were influenced by the Greeks.) In a treatise on architecture, Vitruvius "announced that these buildings should have the proportions of a man." In addition, Vitruvius stated that "a man's body is a model of proportion because with arms or legs extended it fits into those 'perfect' geometrical forms, the square and the circle." Unfortunately, Sir Kenneth writes, we do not know how "the Greek faith in harmonious numbers found expression in their painting and sculpture."

So far, Sir Kenneth has shown that "the discovery of the nude as a form of art is connected with idealism and faith in measurable proportions," but he goes on to write about "other peculiarities of the Greek mind" which furnished the Western world with a pattern of perfection of the human form.

For one thing, Sir Kenneth writes that the Greeks believed that "the body was something to be proud of, and should be kept in perfect form." Obviously, therefore, "[t]he Greeks attached great importance to their nakedness." We see this in the nakedness of the athletes at the Olympic games in ancient Greece.

Another idea of the Greeks, Sir Kenneth writes, is that "the spirit and body are one." Because of this, the Greeks expressed many abstract ideas in terms of the human form. After all, the Greek gods have human form, unlike the Egyptian gods, which were half-animal.

According to Sir Kenneth,

> [...] the nude gains its enduring value from the fact that it reconciles several contrary states. It takes the most sensual and immediately interesting object, the human body, and puts it out of reach of time and desire; it takes the most purely rational concept of which

mankind is capable, mathematical order, and makes it a delight to the senses; and it takes the vague fears of the unknown and sweetens them by showing that the gods are like men and may be worshipped for their life-giving beauty rather than their death-dealing powers.

The place of the nude today is not like what it was in the days of the ancient Greeks. We no longer have "an insatiable appetite for the nude." However, neither "are we likely once more to cut ourselves off from the body, as in the ascetic experience of medieval Christianity." Therefore, the place of the nude today is in the middle of two extremes.

As Sir Kenneth writes, "We are reconciled to the fact that [the body] is our lifelong companion, and since art is concerned with sensory images the scale and rhythm of the body is not easily ignored."

Note: The quotations by Sir Kenneth that appear in this essay are from his book *The Nude: A Study in Ideal Form*.

Chapter 19: Jennifer Jeffers (born 1965): The Politics of Representation

H. Gene Blocker and Sir Kenneth Clark have defended the concept of "high art" as distinct from images in everyday life. However, in her article "The Politics of Representation: The Role of the Gaze in Pornography," Jennifer Jeffers (born 1965) will use a Postmodernist perspective to attack the concept of high art. Indeed, she will argue that men enjoy gazing at the female nude in high art much the same way that men enjoy gazing at naked women in pornography. For Jeffers, there is no relevant distinction between the naked and the nude. Both reflect the objectification of women by a patriarchal society.

The "primary purpose" of her article, Jeffers writes, is "to chart the coordinates of a dominate ideological perspective on the map of Western culture and society." The dominate ideological perspective is patriarchal and can be called "the gaze." According to Jeffers, the gaze is "motivated by a desire to control and attain the object of its desire." The gaze typifies a way of looking at women — it looks at women as objects to be controlled, not as women as autonomous beings. Pornography is one aspect of the gaze, as in pornography women are treated as sexual objects only. However, the nude in fine art is another aspect of the gaze, because once again men enjoy looking at women as objects — in this case, women as idealized objects of beauty.

According to Jeffers, the gaze is an "entire ideology." *The American Heritage Dictionary* defines "ideology" as the "body of ideas reflecting the social needs and aspirations of an individual, class, or culture." In her article, Jeffers uses "ideology" in a wide sense, referring to an entire culture. She writes, "Indeed, the gaze is more than a system or manner of viewing representations of people, the gaze is an entire ideology that governs our behavior, attitude, thinking and, from a larger societal view, our economy and institutions."

I. The Nude, the Naked, and the Gaze

Sir Kenneth Clark made a distinction between the naked and the nude. The naked is an individual, real, unclothed human being, while the nude is an art form that was invented by the ancient Greeks. Sir Kenneth Clark gave a privileged position to the female nude in the history of Western art by making a distinction between high art and low art. According to the distinction made by

Sir Kenneth Clark, the nudes of fine art are an example of high art and are not to be confused with calendars that display pictures of naked women and which, if they are to be called art at all, are examples of low art.

According to Sir Kenneth, there is a boundary between high art and the obscene. For example, in high art the sexuality is supposed to be latent. Once sexual arousal becomes the primary purpose of a piece of "art," it has ceased to be "high" art.

However, Jeffers dismisses the idea of the boundary. According to her, "the boundary exists as a ruse for titillation." The boundary changes as art changes, and artists and other people play with the concept of the boundary, sometimes pushing past the boundary, sometimes staying within the boundary.

For a long time, pornography has been regarded as separate from high art. Indeed, those who are interested in pornography may not be interested in a nude such as the Medici Venus of the first century C.E. Also, as Jeffers points out, the dictionary definition of pornography will tend to keep high art separate from pornography. Often, a dictionary definition will state that pornography has "little or no artistic merit."

However, recently the distinction has become blurred as the male gaze went through a transition. Two factors in this transition were these:

1) Even in the fine arts, depictions of women became "disturbing." Some of the art at this time is what Jeffers calls "fetishized," because it emphasizes the sexual body parts of women, sometimes not even depicting the woman's head.

2) At this time, mass-produced photographs became available. Suddenly, the female nude became the subject of the photographer's camera. Indeed, the advent of pornographic films and videos is an outgrowth of this. Whereas the still camera photographed a "limited set of fantasies," Jeffers writes, now the film or video camera is able to do even more of the "imaginative" work of the male gaze.

II. Desire and the Gaze

What initially creates the male gaze is desire. However, this desire is exploited by Capitalism. One result of Capitalism is the "commodification" of women's bodies, meaning that representations of women's bodies are things (commodities) that can be bought and sold. Capitalism works in part by filling a lack — and Western culture since the time of Plato has perceived sexual desire to be a lack. To be whole, a man needs a woman, and therefore a man without a woman has a lack. Capitalism — as is its wont — rushes to fill this lack with things that can be bought: pictures of naked women in *Playboy* and *Penthouse*, adult movies and videos, and other kinds of pornography.

In doing so, Capitalism exploits both women and men. Women are exploited because it is their bodies that are commodified. However, men are also exploited because Capitalism deals in making money and money cannot be made from such things as love, which can only be freely given. Capitalism can only try to convince both women and men that there is an "ideal" which women must measure up to and which men must possess.

Once women and men have bought into this "ideal," then Capitalism can begin to sell them things. Magazines that derive most of their income from advertisements say that women should be slim, and therefore exercise equipment and diet aids become big business — at the same time fatty fast foods become big business. (If you can sell someone both a fatty hamburger and a diet soft drink, you can continue to make money. The fatty hamburger will ensure that the customer keeps buying the diet soft drink.)

Men are also the targets of advertisements saying that they should consume, yet they should also be slim. (Soft drinks contain large amounts of sugar, yet every actor — and actress — in soft drink commercials is slim.) Indeed, as Jeffers writes about both women and men, "Capitalism creates the ideal, the desire, then it sells you the means to attain it."

In all of this, there is a "binary division" operating in society. We can divide people into the groups of fat and slim. To call someone "fat" is to brand that person with a negative image. This increases the desire of that person to be in the group of the slim.

When it comes to images of women, Jeffers writes, the binary is "the one who sees and the one who is seen." However, this leaves out a third thing: what is *not* seen. Jeffers writes that "what is not seen is the condition or set of conditions that puts the female into the place of object."

In all of this, the gaze has a role: "The role of the gaze ... is to protect the ideology that renders the female invisible as a person and visible as an object."

III. Pornography and the Invisible

Both fine art and pornography are related. According to Jeffers, "The gaze that constructs images of women in art is the same gaze that constructs images of women in pornography."

Today, there is a new presentation of the female form. At one time, in the "high art" of which Clark speaks, the female form was idealized. Today, the female form is "fragmented." In this way of presenting the female form, not all of the female body need be shown — a TV commercial may show only the legs of several women.

Today, pornography is big business; according to Jeffers, it's "a seven billion dollar a year industry in the United States." Pornography has gone beyond the centerfolds of *Playboy* to sadistic adult films featuring women and — illegally — children.

Despite the large number of images of women in 20th-century (and now 21st-century) America, women are still "invisible," according to Jeffers. Women are still invisible in terms of being autonomous persons worthy of respect. Instead, in the representations of women that surround us today, women are merely objects of male desire.

In conclusion, Jeffers writes,

> From the high art ideal of the female nude to the fetishized female body in late twentieth-century Capitalism, the gaze has and continues to "colonize" our sexuality, limit our choices and make invisible the conditions that perpetuate and sustain the gaze's power. The politics of representation constructs an ideology that governs, not only the way we see, but also what we see and even *if* we see certain aspects and people that the gaze wishes to render invisible.

Note: The quotations by Jeffers that appear in this essay are from her essay "The Politics of Representation: The Role of the Gaze in Pornography."

EASTERN PHILOSOPHY

Chapter 20: Mencius (371-circa 289 B.C.E.), Xun Zi (flourished 298-238 B.C.E.), and Dong Zhongshu (circa 179-circa 104 B.C.E.): Three Confucian Theories of Human Nature

A topic that interested ancient Chinese philosophers was human nature. Is there such a thing as human nature, and if there is, what is it? Is human nature good, bad, or indifferent? In this chapter, we see three Chinese philosophers arguing about human nature.

Mencius (371-circa 289 B.C.E.) takes the position that human nature is basically good. Xun Zi (flourished 298-238 B.C.E.) takes the position that human nature is basically bad. Finally, Dong Zhongshu (circa 179-circa 104 B.C.E.) takes a middle position: Human beings are not by nature good, but human nature contains the "seeds" of goodness.

All three Chinese philosophers were followers of Confucius (551-479 BCE), who was a great Chinese teacher and the author of the *Analects*.

Mencius: The Nature of Man is Good

According to Mencius, "All men have the mind which cannot bear [to see the suffering of] others." In other words, all men are basically good. To illustrate this, Mencius uses a famous example. He asks what you would do if you were to see a child suddenly fall into a well. According to Mencius, you would see that the child is in danger of drowning and you would immediately rush to help the child. Furthermore, you would do this without first taking thought about possibly earning a reward. Instead, you would try to help the child simply because your nature is good.

Indeed, according to Mencius, there are four things — the "Four Beginnings" — that all men have:

The feeling of commiseration is the beginning of humanity; the feeling of shame and dislike is the beginning of righteousness; the feeling of deference and compliance is the beginning of propriety;

and the feeling of right and wrong is the beginning of wisdom. Men have these Four Beginnings just as they have their four limbs.

However, merely having the Four Beginnings is not enough — they must be developed if one is to achieve humanity, righteousness, propriety, and wisdom. This is something that everyone — including the ruler — must do.

Mencius' view does not go unchallenged. Kao Tzu's view of human nature is very much different from Mencius' view. According to Kao Tzu, human nature is neither good nor bad; instead, a human being can be made either good or bad. Through proper training [education], a human being can be made good, but through bad training, a human being can be made bad. Human beings are like water. Water can be made to flow East, West, North, or South simply by digging a channel in the direction that you want the water to flow.

Mencius, however, replies that water does have a nature: It always flows downward. According to Mencius, "There is no man without this good nature; neither is there water that does not flow downward." True, one can splash water to make it fly up into the air, but the moment you are done splashing, the water obeys its nature and flows downward once more.

Of course, all of us are aware that some people are good and other people are bad. If human nature is good, why is there this diversity in the goodness of human beings? According to Mencius, "If you let people follow their feelings (original nature), they will be able to do good. This is what is meant by saying that human nature is good. If man does evil, it is not the fault of his natural endowment."

During good times, young people behave well. During bad times, young people behave badly. (The sage behaves well during both good and bad times.) However, Mencius says, the young people's nature is good, but during bad times, they allow their minds "to fall into evil."

This is similar to growing wheat. We plant wheat, and it grows. Some of the wheat is good, because it was planted on good soil and received adequate water. Other wheat is bad, because it was planted on bad soil and did not receive adequate water. The wheat is essentially the same, but its environment affects the way it grows. Similarly, a bad environment can make a good human being bad.

Mencius points out that human beings are essentially alike. Our sense of taste is essentially alike; our sense of hearing is essentially alike; our sense of sight is essentially alike. In general, people can agree on what is a good flavor, what is a pretty sound, and who is a handsome man. Since we are so much alike in our human senses, doesn't it follow that we should be alike when it comes to human nature?

People with essentially good natures do become bad, but that does not mean that they were bad to begin with, Mencius points out. For example, a mountain that used to be forested can become bald if people chop down its trees and start grazing cattle and sheep on the mountain. But that does not mean that the mountain was never forested. Therefore, even if you see a bad person, that does not show that the person was not good to begin with.

Mencius was a good person. If Mencius had to choose between life and righteousness, he said that he will choose righteousness. This does not mean that life is unimportant to him, only that he values righteousness more than life. Other people feel the same way, for if they did not, they would avoid danger at all costs.

A hero can be defined as someone who is willing to risk his or her life in order to save the life of another person; in fact, sometimes heroes die while attempting to save someone else.

One more point: All people are by nature good, so why do some people become great men and other people become small men? Mencius replies, "Those who follow the greater qualities in their nature become great men and those who follow the smaller qualities in their nature become small men."

Of course, this leads to the question of why some people follow the greater qualities while others follow the smaller qualities. According to Mencius, we can be led astray by material things. Instead, we should build up "the nobler part of our nature" first, for if we do so, the inferior part of our nature will not be able to harm us.

Xun Zi: The Nature of Man is Evil

Xun Zi (whose name can also be rendered in English as "Hsun Tzu"), in complete opposition to Mencius, considers the nature of man to be evil. According to him, the goodness of man comes from human activity. That is, a human being is born with evil tendencies, but through education and training — and personal effort — a human being can become good.

To illustrate what he means, Xun Zi uses the examples of crooked wood and blunt metal. In order to straighten crooked wood, you must first heat it and then bend it. In order to sharpen blunt metal (for example, the blunt edge of an ax), you must grind it and whet it. Similarly, in order to make a human being good, you must teach him and discipline him. Thus, both teachers and laws are necessary for human beings to become good.

According to Xun Zi, the sage-kings of antiquity realized that human nature is evil and therefore they "created the rules of propriety and instituted laws and systems" so that men could become superior men. Superior men follow the rules of propriety and obey the rules of the realm, while inferior men let their passions run wild.

There is a difference between human nature and human activity, according to Xun Zi. Man's nature is something that we have no control over — we cannot learn it. However, we can learn to have propriety and to have righteousness.

The nature of man is evil, as can be shown by man's desires. Anyone who is hungry desires to eat. However, although a hungry person in Chinese society wants to eat, if he sees some elders ahead of him, he will wait for them to eat in order to show them respect. In addition, a younger brother will take over the work of an older brother in order to show the older brother respect.

Of course, one may ask the question, "If man's nature is evil, whence come propriety and righteousness?" Xun Zi answers that propriety and righteousness come from "the activity of sages." So once more, activity results in propriety and righteousness — these qualities are not a part of human nature. So if some brothers decide to divide their property, if they follow the nature they were born with, each of them will try to grab the largest share. But if they have been taught well, they will divide the property fairly.

According to Xun Zi, "People desire to be good because their nature is evil." By this, he means that evil is a lack, and people wish to fill their lacks. If people are ugly, they wish to be handsome. If people have low status, they wish to have high status. If people are poor, they wish to be rich. So, since people have an evil character, they wish to be good. (If people were already good, they would not wish to be good.)

However, because people's nature is evil, we need civilization. We need rules of propriety, laws, a ruler, and punishments for crimes. Without these things, according to Xun Zi, "The whole world would be in violence and disorder and all would perish in an instant." (In many ways, Xun Zi is like Thomas Hobbes, who also felt that without laws, a ruler, and punishments for crimes, the world would fall into chaos.

Lest someone should think that Xun Zi is too pessimistic, here is his answer to the question, "Shall we consider humanity, righteousness, laws, and correct principles as basically impossible to be known or practiced?" According to Xun Zi, people can know these things. The sages have learned them, and so can other people. If they do not learn them, it is because they do not wish to learn them.

Dong Zhongshu: Man's Nature is Neither Good Nor Evil

Dong Zhongshu takes a middle position between the positions of Mencius and of Xun Zi. According to Dong Zhongshu, "In his real character man has both humanity (*ren*) and greed." Man receives his character from Heaven, and Heaven also has opposing forces — the yin and the yang — so we should not be surprised that man also has opposing forces.

Many Chinese philosophers draw comparisons from nature, and Dong Zhongshu is no exception. He compares man's nature to rice stalks and goodness to rice because rice comes out of a rice stalk, but not all of the rice stalk becomes rice. Similarly, goodness comes out of a person's nature, but not all nature becomes goodness. Dong Zhongshu also compares man's nature to eyes because when a person's eyes are closed he cannot see. A man's nature before he becomes good is like an eye that has been closed. It takes training before a man's nature can be opened to goodness.

In addition, Dong Zhongshu compares man's nature to a silk cocoon or an egg. Before the egg becomes a chicken, it must be hatched, and before a silk cocoon can be made into silk it must be unravelled. Similarly, a man's nature "needs to be trained before becoming good."

Because of these comparisons, Dong Zhongshu concludes, "Therefore goodness has to do with training and not to do with nature."

This brings up the question, "Since nature contains the beginning of goodness and since the mind possesses the basic substance of goodness, how can nature not be regarded as good?" Dong Zhongshu answers that the silk cocoon contains only potential silk and that the egg contains only a potential chicken. Therefore, a person's nature contains only potential goodness. To make the goodness actual takes training.

Dong Zhongshu uses a high standard of goodness — the standard of the Sage. To be good, one must achieve the standard of the Sage. Because of this, Dong Zhongshu's evaluation of life and nature differs from the evaluation made by Mencius. Mencius thought that people are good by nature, but Dong Zhongshu thinks people become good through training.

Note: The quotations by Chinese philosophers that appear in this essay are from *A Source Book in Chinese Philosophy*, translated by Wing-tsit Chan.

Chapter 21: The Path of Yoga

The *Bhagavad Gita* (Sanskit meaning "Song of the Lord") is one of the sacred works of India. It is taken from Book 6 of the very long epic work *Mahabharata*, which has about 100,000 verses. In the *Bhagavad Gita*, Arjuna — the son of a king — is on the verge of going to war. His charioteer is Krishna, who is the incarnation of the god Vishnu (the Preserver). The whole of the *Bhagavad Gita* consists of a dialogue between Arjuna and Krishna. Arjuna asks questions, and Krishna answers them.

As one of the sacred books of Hinduism, the *Bhagavad Gita* has several ideas that form its intellectual background. These ideas include belief in:

- Reincarnation. The Hindus believe that all of us, except those who achieve enlightenment, will be reincarnated over and over again. We die, but then we live again in another body. We will be reincarnated as a human being, or as an animal.

- Karma. Through our actions and deeds, we acquire karma, which will determine what we shall come back as in our next incarnation. If our deeds are good, we will come back as a human being of high status. If our deeds are bad, we will come back as an animal of low status.

- The Wish for the Extinction of Desire. In the West, human beings usually want personal immortality. They hope to have an afterlife so that they can continue to love others and to acquire knowledge. Often, in the East, human beings wish to escape from the bonds of desire. The desire is to escape from the bonds of karma and reincarnation.

- Yoga. Yoga is a practice that will lead to the extinction of desire. There are two forms of yoga — the yoga of knowledge and the yoga of action — that are described below. In the *Bhagavad Gita*, Krishna tells Arjuna about the yoga of action.

Wikipedia defines "yoga" in this way:

Yoga is a group of physical, mental, and spiritual practices or disciplines which originated in ancient India and aim to control and still the mind, recognizing a detached witness-consciousness untouched by the mind and mundane suffering.

The Path of Yoga

At the beginning of the *Bhagavad Gita*, Arjuna is filled with sorrow because he does not want to fight in a civil war. However, Krishna tells him,

"Don't be a coward, Arjuna.
"It doesn't become you at all.
"Shake off your weakness and rise!"
Arjuna then asks:
"How can I fight Bhishma and Drona [his rivals],
"fitter objects for my veneration?"
Krishna replies:
"You mourn those, Arjuna, who do not deserve mourning.
"The learned mourn neither the living nor the dead."

One reason why the learned mourn neither the living nor the dead is because the Self lives on despite the state of the body.
According to Krishna,

"How utterly strange that bodies are said to be destroyed
"when the immutable, illimitable and indestructible Self lives on!"

Because of this, Krishna asks,

"... how can [a man] possibly kill, or make another kill?"

Krishna sums up his main point in this way:

"This embodied Self, Arjuna, is imperishable,
"You have no reason to grieve for any natural creature."

Then Krishna speaks about the "truths of action." One way to break the "fetters of karma" is through the path of knowledge; the other way is through the path of action. To walk the path of action, one must

> "[...] give up attachment, be indifferent to failure and success. [...]
> "With this mental poise,
> "you shall release yourself from evil and good deeds."

Much Eastern philosophy assumes that we are reincarnated over and over again. What you do in this life will determine what or who you will come back as in the next life. The goal of the individual is to not come back at all, but instead to break the cycle of continually being reborn and to eliminate all desires.

Arjuna then asks,

> "Who is the man of poise, Krishna?
> "Who is steady in devotion?
> "How does he speak, rest, walk?"

Krishna replies by saying that the man of poise is that person who

> "[...] has shed all desire;
> "he is content in the Self by the Self.
> "He is steady. He endures sorrow.
> "He does not chase pleasure.
> "Affection, anger and fear do not touch him.
> "He is not selfish.
> "He does not rejoice in prosperity.
> "He is not saddened by want.
> "He can recall his senses from their objects
> "as the tortoise pulls in its head.
> "Objects scatter away from the good but lazy man,
> "but desire remains.
> "In the perfect state, however, desire also goes."

The Yoga of Action

Arjuna then asks,

"If, as you say, Krishna, knowledge exceeds action,
"why do you urge me to this terrible war?"

Krishna replies by pointing out two ways of living life. The way you should live your life depends on the kind of person you are, but both ways involve yoga. One way of leading life — best for contemplative people — is the yoga of knowledge; the other way of leading life — best for active people — is the yoga of action. Both ways of leading life are suitable and lead to God. However, if one chooses to follow the yoga of action, one's actions must be selfless. Therefore, Krishna advises Arjuna to

"[...] work, but work selflessly.
"All deeds are traps, except ritual deeds.
"Hence the need for selfless action."

The yogi (a person who practices yoga) of action is known as the karma yogi. A person who was a karma yogi in his life was Mahatma Gandhi (1869-1948). According to his secretary, Gandhi called the *Bhagavad Gita* his "spiritual reference work."

Louis Fischer's book *Gandhi: His Life and Message for the World*, quotes Gandhi's definition of the "perfect karma yogi":

He is a devotee who is jealous of none, who is a fount of mercy, who is without egotism, who is selfless, who treats alike cold and heat, happiness and misery, who is ever forgiving, who is always contented, whose resolutions are firm, who has dedicated mind and soul to God, who causes no dread, who is not afraid of others, who is free from exultation, sorrow and fear, who is pure, who is versed in action yet remains unaffected by it, who renounces all fruit, good or bad, who treats friend and foe alike, who is untouched by respect or disrespect, who is not puffed up by praise, who does not go under when people speak ill of him, who loves silence and solitude, who has a disciplined reason. Such devotion is inconsistent with the existence at the same time of strong attachments.

All of the above Gandhi was able to sum up with one word: "Selflessness."

Note: The quotations from the *Bhagavad Gita* that appear in this essay were translated by P. Lal.

Chapter 22: Lao Tzu (circa 604 B.C.E.): The Tao Te Ching

Taoism is intended to be a practical philosophy — one that you can apply in your everyday life. Therefore, in reading the main book of Taoism, *Tao Te Ching*, written by Lao Tzu (circa 604 B.C.E.), you can ask yourself, "What does this mean to me? How can I get in touch with Nature and achieve happiness?"

Let's take a look at section 63 of the *Tao Te Ching*:

Act without action.
Do without ado.
Taste without tasting.
Whether it is big or small, many or few, repay hatred with virtue.
Prepare for the difficult while it is still easy.
Deal with the big while it is still small.
Difficult undertakings have always started with what is easy,
And great undertakings have always started with what is small.
Therefore the sage never strives for the great,
And thereby the great is achieved.
He who makes rash promises surely lacks faith.
He who takes things too easily will surely encounter much difficulty.
For this reason the sage regards things as difficult,
And therefore he encounters no difficulty.

Here we find advice about great undertakings. Since many readers of this book will have as their current great undertaking getting a college diploma — to be followed by the great undertaking of getting and keeping a job — let's look at how two students approach studying. One student is a fool, and the other student is a Taoist.

The fool comes late to class — if he even attends class — seldom takes notes, and does not keep up with the reading. When the fool is assigned a 20-page term paper due at the end of the quarter, he says to himself or herself, "Hey, that's a couple of months away! I've got lots of time to write that paper.

So I'm going to have fun now, and I'll write the paper later." (This is the fool's rash promise to himself or herself.)

Time flies by, and suddenly it's finals week! The fool suddenly realizes that he or she hasn't started the paper and he has a D- in the class so far. The fool asks the professor for an incomplete, but the professor — who takes attendance and knows the student has been blowing off the class — declines. Now the fool has to study for his or her finals and write a 20-page term paper at the same time.

All teachers, unfortunately, have known fools. Because of the fools, teachers take attendance in an attempt to force the fool — for his or her own good — to attend class. Teachers also are aware that at the end of the quarter or semester the fool will end up working harder than anyone else in the class — and learn the least from their hard work.

In his book *Mere Christianity*, C. S. Lewis writes,

> Teachers will tell you that the laziest boy in the class is the one who works hardest in the end. They mean this. If you give two boys, say, a proposition in geometry to do, the one who is prepared to take trouble will try to understand it. The lazy boy will try to learn it by heart because, for the moment, that needs less effort. But six months later, when they are preparing for an exam, that lazy boy is doing hours and hours of miserable drudgery over things the other boy understands, and positively enjoys, in a few minutes. Laziness means more work in the long run.

The Taoist student, in contrast to the fool, attends every class, takes good notes, and keeps up with the reading. After all, the Taoist student realizes that graduating can require a great effort. When the Taoist student hears about the 20-page term paper, she immediately begins work on the paper.

However, she does not try to write the entire paper in a few days — the way the fool is forced to. Instead, the Taoist student first finds a topic that she is interested in and that the teacher will accept as the topic for her term paper. (The fool has to start researching the first topic that comes to his mind, even if it bores him — as it probably will.) Then the Taoist student breaks the process down into small steps that anyone can do. Week by week, she researches and writes her paper, learning about an interesting topic in the process and ensuring herself a good grade as well.

When the fool is desperately trying to come up with a topic to research, the Taoist student is finishing the proofreading of her paper.

That is the way that Taoists approach great undertakings. The undertaking appears overwhelming, but if you work on it little by little, the task gets done.

According to Annie Dillard, author of *Pilgrim at Tinker Creek*, "You know when you think about writing a book, you think it is overwhelming. But, actually, you break it down into tiny little tasks any moron can do."

Of course, we all know of students who get good grades without learning anything. Sometimes they cheat. Does this mean the Taoist student is a fool?

No. One purpose of college is to acquire job skills. Good grades can help you get your first job, but good skills are what will keep you from being fired. One of my correspondence students in philosophy wrote me about a computer-programming course that she and a friend had taken. The course was difficult, and my student was having a hard time. The final project was to do some computer programming — everyone in the class had to do the same project.

Guess what? A computer programming whiz in the class finished the programming project early and offered to give a copy of it to any other student in the class who wanted it. My student said, No, and received an F in the class. She had to take the class over. My student's friend said, Yes, and received an A in the class.

Later, both students got jobs. The friend who had cheated and received an A was fired because her boss quickly discovered that she didn't know how to program a computer. My student who had received an F and had to take the class over kept her job — in fact, she made a copy of her paycheck and mailed it to the friend who cheated!

This doesn't mean that the Taoist student is a grind who never enjoys life. Taoists probably enjoy life more than anyone else. They do the work for the day, then go out and have fun. In fact, they enjoy their fun better than other people because their work for the day is done. In addition, they enjoy the process of doing their work. Taoist students tend to enjoy their classes because they understand what the professor is talking about — they've kept up with the work and so the professor does not appear to be speaking in a foreign language.

However, if a Taoist student finds himself or herself not enjoying his major, he or she will change majors.

Taoists believe that at one time Humankind lived in harmony with Nature, but that since then Humankind has grown away from Nature, resulting in many problems. For example, in the United States today is an epidemic of obesity. Department stores are beginning to carry shirts in XXL and XXXL sizes because people can't squeeze their excess flesh into XL shirts anymore.

Why is this happening? One answer is the proliferation of fast food restaurants, which serve fatty hamburgers and greasy french fries. (A TV commercial for low-calorie food or exercise equipment will probably be sandwiched between two TV commercials for fast food.) One hundred years ago, Americans ate mostly grains, fruits, and vegetables. Today the emphasis is on animal fat. For example, take Dave Thomas, founder of Wendy's. He ate at Wendy's — just look at what it did to his midsection. (Wendy's TV commercials that showed Dave's big belly do have truth in advertising.)

To lose weight, remember the laws of Nature. You know that more food and less exercise means weight gain, so if you want to lose weight, try less food and more exercise. (And if you think you can gobble mass quantities of pizza and drink mass quantities of beer and not gain weight, weigh yourself now and weigh yourself when you graduate — the fiendish laughter you will hear in the distance will be mine.)

A true Taoist has an interesting way of dealing with obesity. He or she never becomes obese in the first place.

Read the *Tao Te Ching* and find out what it has to say to you.

Note: The quotations by Lao Tzu that appear in this essay are from *The Way of Lao Tzu*, translated by Wing-tsit Chan.

Chapter 23: Benjamin Hoff (born 1946): The Tao of Pooh

The Tao of Pooh, by Benjamin Hoff. New York: Penguin Books, 1982. 158 pages.

The Tao of Pooh is a strange little, funny little, happy little book. In a way, it's a self-help book, since Hoff says that "it's about how to stay happy and calm under any circumstances." But actually, it's much more than that, for it's a book of applied philosophy.

The particular philosophy discussed in *The Tao of Pooh* is Taoism, which Hoff calls much more than a philosophy, as it's a way of life. In the introductory chapter, "The *How* of Pooh," Hoff explains Taoism by contrasting it with two other Eastern philosophies: Confucianism and Buddhism.

Hoff asks us to imagine a copy of a Chinese painting of *The Vinegar Tasters*. This allegorical painting shows three men sampling vinegar. Each has dipped his finger in a vat of vinegar and placed it in his mouth.

The first man, K'ung Fu-tse (Confucius), has a sour look on his face because "he believed that the present was out of step with the past, and that the government of man on earth was out of harmony with the Way of Heaven, the government of the universe."

The second man, Buddha, has a bitter look on his face because to him, "life on earth was bitter, filled with attachments and desires that led to suffering." He saw the world as "a setter of traps, a generator of illusions, a revolving wheel of pain for all creatures."

In contrast to these two men, the third man, Lao-tse (author of the *Tao Te Ching*, the oldest book on Taoism), is smiling because he knows that "the harmony that naturally existed between heaven and earth from the very beginning could be found by anybody at any time. ... To Lao-tse, the world was not a setter of traps but a teacher of valuable lessons. Its lessons needed to be learned, just as its laws needed to be followed; then all would go well."

So, what does this have to do with Winnie the Pooh, a "dumpy little bear that wanders around asking silly questions, making up songs, and going through all kinds of adventures, without ever accumulating any amount of intellectual knowledge or losing his simpleminded sort of happiness"? The answer: According to Hoff, Winnie the Pooh is a great Western master of Taoism, exemplifying Taoism in his everyday life, which is exactly where it ought to be exemplified.

For example, in chapter 2, "The Tao of *Who*?" Hoff uses Pooh to explain the principle of the Uncarved Block (which Hoff jokes was named after Pooh, being *P'u* in Chinese). According to Hoff, "The essence of the principle of the Uncarved Block is that things in their original simplicity contain their own natural power, power that is easily spoiled and lost when that simplicity is changed. [...] From the state of the Uncarved Block comes the ability to enjoy the simple and the quiet, the natural and the plain. Along with that comes the ability to do things spontaneously and have them work, odd as that may appear to others at times."

Throughout *The Tao of Pooh*, Hoff quotes from the Winnie the Pooh books to show the principles of Taoism in action. After all, it is Pooh who is the hero of the books: Pooh finds the North Pole, finds Eeyore's lost tail, finds his and Piglet's way home when they get lost in the woods, and rescues Roo when the baby kangaroo falls in the river. And it is Pooh who creates his hums, and who is always ready to wish everyone a Happy Thursday (even if he can't spell it).

Hoff also criticizes the other characters of the Pooh books for their non-Taoist tendencies. In doing so, he engages in some legitimate social criticism. For example, in the "Busy Backson" chapter, he criticizes the American tendency to be like Rabbit, always rushing about, usually to no good purpose. Instead, why not sit down to a picnic lunch and *relax* a little?

Hoff says: "You see them almost everywhere you go, it seems. On practically any sunny sort of day, you can see the Backsons stampeding through the park, making all kinds of loud breathing noises. Perhaps you are enjoying a picnic on the grass when you suddenly look up to find that one or two of them just ran over your lunch."

An example of our Busy Backson society is the Hamburger Stand. Other societies have places where people sit, consume light food, and talk for hours. But our fast-food places, besides poisoning the customers' health, are in the business of turning over items fast. The customer buys food, consumes it quickly, and goes, leaving his seat for the next consumer of dead animal products.

Also, American society believes in the Great Reward: Work hard, run yourself to death, and someday (but not just yet) you'll receive a Great Reward. Taoism doesn't believe in running yourself to death now for a Great Reward in the future. Instead: Be happy today; enjoy the process of whatever it is that you do; everyone's favorite day should be Today.

THE MEANING OF LIFE

Chapter 24: Meaning Without God: Can Life Without God Be Meaningful?

Can life without God be meaningful?

There are two answers to this question: yes and no. The "no" answer becomes apparent in Bertrand Russell's description of the universe as presented to us by modern science. In his book *A Free Man's Worship (Mysticism and Logic)*, Russell first quotes a passage stating that the universe was created by a heartless being, and then he continues,

> Such, in outline, but even more purposeless, more void of meaning, is the world which Science presents for our belief. Amid such a world, if anywhere, our ideals henceforward must find a home. That man is the product of causes which had no prevision of the end they were achieving; that his origin, his growth, his hopes and fears, his loves and beliefs, are but the outcome of accidental collocations of atoms; that no fire, no heroism, no intensity of thought and feeling, can preserve an individual life beyond the grave; that all the labours of the ages, all the devotion, all the inspirations, all the noonday brightness of human genius, are destined to extinction in the vast death of the solar system, and that the whole temple of Man's achievement must inevitably be buried beneath the debris of a universe in ruins — all these things, if not quite beyond dispute, are yet so nearly certain, that no philosophy which rejects them can hope to stand. Only within the scaffolding of these truths, only on the firm foundation of unyielding despair, can the soul's habitation henceforth be safely built.

Given this kind of universe, many people will say that life has no meaning and seek to find refuge in God — a Being that Russell believes does not exist. However, Russell continues and finds some meaning in life without God:

Brief and powerless is Man's life; on him and all his race the slow, sure doom falls pitiless and dark. Blind to good and evil, reckless of destruction, omnipotent matter rolls on its relentless way; for Man, condemned today to lose his dearest, tomorrow himself to pass through the gate of darkness, it remains only to cherish, ere yet the blow falls, the lofty thoughts that ennoble his little day; disdaining the coward terrors of the slave of Fate, to worship at the shrine that his own hands have built; undismayed by the empire of chance, to preserve a mind free from the wanton tyranny that rules his outward life; proudly defiant of the irresistible forces that tolerate, for a moment, his knowledge and his condemnation, to sustain alone, a weary but unyielding Atlas, the world that his own ideals have fashioned despite the trampling march of unconscious power.

Russell has certainly painted an unromantic picture of the universe; however, we know that he found meaning in his existence on earth despite his lack of belief in God and in an afterlife. Russell found his meaning first in mathematics and philosophy, and later in his opposition to the atomic bomb. For much of his life, he was in opposition to war. Certainly in this world there are evils to be fought and new knowledge to be discovered. I believe that Norse mythology also presents a picture of a universe that will ultimately end in chaos, but is yet a universe in which there are gods who find meaning in their lives by struggling mightily and heroically to stave off the final destruction of the universe.

In Norse mythology, Ragnarok is the name given to the twilight of the gods and the destruction of the universe. Ragnarok will be preceded by the coming of three straight winters with no intervening summers. These will be followed by three more winters, during which wars will be fought on earth. Three great monsters that the Norse gods had previously bound will break free and will attack the gods, riding over the rainbow bridge named Bifrost into the domain of the gods. The wolf Fenris will kill the chief god Odin, but will in turn be killed by Odin's son Vidar. Another son of Odin, Thor, will kill the Midgard serpent, which is so big that it encircles the earth, but Thor will die from the serpent's venom. The watchman of the gods, Heimdall, will fight the evil Loki until both are killed. The god Freyr, who cares for the fruits of the earth, will be killed by Surtur, who will then burn up the universe.

So, the gods know that the universe will end in destruction, but rather than despairing, they devote their efforts to postponing the day of destruction known as Ragnarok. Odin is the chief god responsible for postponing the day of destruction. He values wisdom. In one myth, he went to the Well of Wisdom and begged its guardian, Mimir the Wise, for a drink from it. In payment, Mimir, who was blind, asked Odin for one of his eyes. Odin paid this price. Perching on Odin's shoulders are two ravens, Thought (Hugin) and Memory (Munin), which fly over the world and bring Odin the information they discover.

Odin was always a benefactor to Humankind. He won the knowledge of the Runes by suffering for it in a kind of crucifixion, and he gave this knowledge to Humankind. In addition, he took from the Giants the skaldic mead, which made a poet of anyone who drank from it, and he gave this mead to Humankind.

Despite the view that the universe cares nothing for human endeavors and that the universe will eventually kill Humankind, Bertrand Russell and the Norse gods found meaning in their lives. That meaning lay in serving Humankind and in staving off the day of destruction as long as possible.

Chapter 25: Viktor Frankl (1905-1997): Man's Search for Meaning

Viktor Frankl. *Man's Search for Meaning*. New York: Pocket Books, 1959.

I hope that one result of the success of the movie *Schindler's List* is that many more people begin to read literature about the Holocaust — I know I have.

One excellent book about the Holocaust is *Man's Search for Meaning* by Viktor E. Frankl. Frankl was a neurophysician who was sent to Auschwitz and other concentration camps simply because he was a Jew. Since he was also a psychiatrist, he was able to observe concentration camp life — despite being plagued by apathy like other prisoners — and later write about life in the concentration camps from a psychological standpoint. In addition, he developed logotherapy — an important form of psychiatry — after suffering for years in concentration camps.

Man's Search for Meaning is divided into two parts. The first part is a short autobiography of his experiences in the concentration camps, and the second part is a brief explication of logotherapy. In addition, there is a brief postscript and a long bibliography. The essay you are now reading focuses on the short autobiography.

Frankl describes the psychological development of the concentration camp prisoner in three parts: 1) the period following admission, 2) the period when the prisoner is well entrenched in camp routines, and 3) the period following release and liberation.

The First Period: Following Admission

The first period is when the prisoner is admitted into the concentration camp and first begins to learn what is in store for him. Some characteristics of this period include:

Shock.

The first period can be characterized as a time of shock. The prisoners lost nearly all of their material possessions and were separated from their loved ones. Prisoners were made to strip, then they were shorn of their hair — including pubic hair — and finally they were sent to the showers. If they were lucky, water came from the showerheads; if they were unlucky, poison gas came from the showerheads.

Whether a prisoner survived the first day or not was at the whim of an SS officer. Frankl describes how he was made to go either to the left or to the right at the discretion of an SS officer. One side meant death; the other meant life as a laborer. As the prisoners filed past the SS officer, he would look them over and decide whether they would be saved to do work or would be exterminated immediately.

When Frankl came to the SS officer, "The SS man looked me over, appeared to hesitate, then put both his hands on my shoulders. I tried very hard to look smart, and he turned my shoulders very slowly until I faced right, and I moved over to that side." Most of the people in line were sent to the left, and they were killed.

Grim Sense of Humor, and Curiosity.

Other characteristics of this period were a grim sense of humor, and curiosity. The humor came in relief that real water flowed from the showerheads. The curiosity was about what would happen next.

The Second Period: Well Entrenched in Camp Routine

The second period occurs when the prisoner is well entrenched in camp routine. At this point, Frankl refers to Dostoevski's definition of a human as "a being who can get used to anything." The prisoners very quickly discovered that Dostoevski's definition is true. After all, they grew used to sleeping several to a bunk under two thin blankets, and even people who used to awaken at the slightest sound were now sleeping soundly due to exhaustion. Still, there were those who committed suicide by running into the electrically charged barbed wire that ran around the concentration camp. Frankl had to promise himself not to run into the wire.

The following paragraphs describe some of the characteristics of this second period.

Deprivation of Human Dignity.

Frankl gives several vivid examples of this. One tells about cleaning the ditches that served as latrines in the camps. Prisoners would be forced to shovel the human excrement into wheelbarrows, then remove it to a more remote location. Should any excrement fly into the air and fall onto the prisoner's face, the prisoner was forbidden to remove it and would be beaten if he tried.

In another example, Frankl was in a work party mending a railway track, when he stopped working for a minute. The guard saw him, thought he was loafing and threw a pebble at him to get his attention. Frankl writes, "That, to me, seemed the way to attract the attention of a beast, to call a domestic animal back to its job, a creature with which you have so little in common that you do not even punish it."

Blunting of Human Emotions, Apathy, and Emotional Deprivation.

Frankl gives two vivid examples of prisoners with these characteristics. First, a 12-year-old boy suffered from frostbite. A prisoner who had become accustomed to the camp routine watched unmoved as the camp doctor broke off with tweezers the boy's blackened, frozen toes. Second, after a prisoner had died in the camp, it was not unusual for other prisoners to look the body over to see if there was anything that they could use. Thus, a prisoner who thought that the dead man's shoes were better than his would exchange shoes with the dead man.

Starvation.

Frankl writes, "When the last layers of our subcutaneous fat had vanished and we looked like skeletons disguised with skin and rags, we could watch our bodies begin to devour themselves. The organism digested its own protein, and the muscles disappeared. Then the body had no powers of resistance left."

Religious Interest.

Many prisoners developed a very sincere religion. In addition, Frankl noticed, "Sensitive people who were used to a rich intellectual life may have suffered much pain (they were often of a delicate constitution), but the damage to their inner selves was less. They were able to retreat from their terrible surroundings to a life of inner riches and spiritual freedom." Furthermore, prisoners sometimes experienced beauty as the result of their intense inner life. For example, once a prisoner rushed into Frankl's hut and urged everyone to come outside to watch a beautiful sunset.

Love.

One way that Frankl was able to sustain himself was through his love for his young wife, who did not survive the Holocaust. Often, he imagined himself talking to his wife and he imagined his wife answering him. Through these imaginary conversations, Frankl was able to survive the harsh conditions of the concentration camps. In a powerful scene, when Frankl believes that he may die, he tells a fellow prisoner a message to give to his (Frankl's) wife: "Listen, Otto, if I don't get back home to my wife, and if you should see her again, then tell her that I talked of her daily, hourly. You remember. Secondly, I have loved her more than anyone. Thirdly, the short time I have been married to her outweighs everything, even all we have gone through here."

Freedom.

Many people might think that the prisoners had no freedom, that their freedom was taken away from them when they entered the concentration camp. Frankl, however, believes that people have the freedom to choose the attitude they take to their suffering. For example, in a concentration camp, one person's response to suffering was to act like a beast. Another person's response was to act like a saint. Frankl writes, "In the final analysis it becomes clear that the sort of person the prisoner became was the result of an inner decision, and not the result of camp influences alone."

Two Races of Men.

One might expect that all the camp guards were brutal; indeed, many of them were, but some did perform acts of kindness, such as giving a prisoner a piece of bread and a kind word. Even among the guards were kind people.

According to Frankl,

> From all this we may learn that there are two races of men in this world, but only these two — the 'race' of the decent man and the 'race' of the indecent man. Both are found everywhere; they penetrate into all groups of society. No group consists of decent or indecent people. In this sense, no group is of 'pure race' — and therefore one occasionally found a decent fellow among the camp guards. Life in a concentration camp tore open the human soul and exposed its depths.

The Future.

Frankl believes that humans live by looking toward the future because he discovered that the prisoner who lost faith in his future was doomed. He writes, "I remember two cases of would-be suicide. ... Both used the typical argument — they had nothing more to expect from life. In both cases it was a question of getting them to realize that life was still expecting something from them; something in the future was expected of them."

The Third Period: Following Release and Liberation

The third period occurred when the prisoner was freed from the concentration camp. Here are some characteristics of this period:

Not at First Pleased.

Surprisingly, the prisoner did not feel pleasure and happiness immediately after being released. It took him time to learn how to feel pleasure and happiness again. Frankl writes, "We had literally lost the ability to feel pleased and had to relearn it slowly."

Slow Process Back to Becoming Human Again.

Many people felt bitterness because of what they had lost while they were in the concentration camps. Some used this bitterness to justify transgressions against others as when a former prisoner walked across a field and destroyed young stalks of oats, justifying his action by saying, "... hasn't enough been taken from us? My wife and my child have been gassed — not to mention everything else — and you would forbid me to tread on a few stalks of oats!" Frankl adds, "Only slowly could these men be guided back to the commonplace truth that no one has the right to do wrong, not even if wrong has been done to them. We had to strive to lead them back to the truth ...."

In conclusion, Frankl writes, "The crowning experience of all, for the homecoming man, is the wonderful feeling that, after all he has suffered, there is nothing he need fear any more — except his God."

Note: This essay is based in part on a lecture outline handed out by Ohio University philosophy professor Dr. Donald Borchert in his course "Stories and the Pursuit of Meaning." In his handout, Dr. Borchert summarized the first part of Frankl's book.

Chapter 26: Viktor Frankl (1905-1997): Logotherapy

Viktor Frankl (1905-1997) is famous as the author of *Man's Search for Meaning*, which consists of two parts: The first part is a short autobiographical account of his years spent in German concentration camps during World War II, while the second part is a short explanation of a theory of therapy centering on human meaning that Frankl developed in part as a response to his concentration camp experiences. This essay focuses on the second part of Frankl's book.

Autobiography

First, I will sum up the conclusions Frankl reached as a result of his concentration camp experiences. Most importantly, Frankl concluded that we are free — even if we are in a concentration camp. Frankl believes that we are free within a situation. We are always free to choose our attitude toward the situation we are in. Even if we are in front of a firing squad, we can choose our attitude: We can say, "I'm guilty; I deserve to die," or we can scream, "You dirty sons of bitches! I damn you to hell!"

Frankl reached the conclusion that we are free after observing the actions of his fellow prisoners in the concentration camps. Some people acted like swine, while other people acted like saints. Some people became brutal camp guards, while other people gave away their last crust of bread and comforted other prisoners.

Frankl pointed out that even in the concentration camp, there were always choices to make. For example, an important choice Frankl and the other prisoners were confronted with was whether to commit suicide. An electric fence ran around the concentration camps and one could commit suicide by running into the electric fence.

In addition, Frankl learned how important it is to have meaning in your life. Those people who lost hope in the future soon died. But those who had something to look forward to (a child waiting for them outside the concentration camp, or scientific work which could be done only by the prisoner) were able — in many cases — to survive the concentration camp.

The Will to Meaning

In his logotherapy, Frankl concentrates on the Will to Meaning. We are free, and we have goals and ideals. These goals and ideals do not fit the deterministic model of If A, then B. (Determinism is a philosophical theory that we never act freely — whatever we do has been determined by forces beyond our control.) Instead, these goals and ideals are future possibilities that we can decide to strive to make actual. Frankl believes that we are "pulled" by our goals and ideals — not pushed from behind as in the deterministic model. According to Frankl, "Man is never driven to moral behavior; in each instance he decides to behave morally." In other words, moral behavior is an act of freedom.

Existential Frustration and Noögenic Neurosis

Frankl believes that if one's will to meaning is frustrated, the result can be noögenic neurosis. A neurosis is "a functional disorder of the mind or emotions with no obvious physical cause." Noös refers to mind or spirit, and so a noögenic neurosis is a neurosis of the mind or spirit arising from existential frustration.

For example, a high-ranking American official began seeing a psychotherapist; later he came to Frankl. Frankl discovered that the official with very unhappy with American foreign policy, and that this was frustrating the official's will to meaning. Therefore, Frankl suggested that the official find another job — the official did so, and his problems cleared up immediately.

Noö-Dynamics

According to Frankl, a certain amount of tension in one's life is normal. There should be a tension between what one has already achieved and what one has left to achieve, and a tension between what one already is and what one should become. Life in the land of the lotus-eaters is not a life for a human being, according to Frankl.

The Existential Vacuum

As a result of several surveys, Frankl has discovered that an existential vacuum exists in the lives of many people. For many people, life has no meaning. As long as they are busy, they do not recognize the lack of meaning in their lives, but when Sunday comes, they suddenly have nothing to do and recognize that their life consists of busywork. According to Frankl, "The existential vacuum manifests itself mainly in a state of boredom."

The Meaning of Life

However, one can discover a meaning (or meanings) in one's life, and Frankl gives several suggestions for finding this meaning. But first, he states that the meaning of life always changes. There is no one meaning to life. Asking someone for the meaning to life is like asking a chess grandmaster what is the best move in chess. The best move depends on the situation, and so does the meaning one finds in life.

However, Frankl gives us three ways to discover the meaning that one's life holds (or can hold) for one. First, one can find meaning in life by doing a deed. A career can have meaning. One can start a homeless shelter, or write a book, or graduate from college, etc.

Second, one can find meaning in life by experiencing a value. The value can be experiencing a work of art or culture. Some people devote themselves to the study of Shakespeare. Others find meaning in life through travel. Another way to find meaning in life by experiencing a value is by experiencing someone — that is, being in love. One's devotion to a spouse can bring meaning to one's life.

Third, one can find meaning in life by suffering. This shows the influence of Frankl's concentration camp experience upon his logotherapy. If one is faced with unavoidable suffering, one can respond bravely to the suffering. (Of course, if the suffering is avoidable, then one ought to avoid it.) Someone who has incurable cancer can respond bravely to the cancer.

An example of finding meaning by suffering is that of a man whose wife had died. He had loved her very much, and he suffered very much after her death. Frankl asked the man what would have happened if the man had died first instead of his wife. The man responded that his wife would have suffered very much. The man then realized that by surviving his wife he had spared her the tremendous suffering that he was now experiencing. This gave his suffering a meaning.

Modern Collective Neurosis: Nihilism

Frankl also addresses what he calls the modern collective neurosis — that is, nihilism, or the idea that life has no meaning. Everywhere it seems that scientists and other people are trying to deny Humankind's freedom. Many people seem to believe that Humankind is "nothing but" a body that responds to physical laws the same way that a rock or a planet does. Many people seem to believe that Humankind is no more free than a rock or a planet.

However, Frankl believes that Humankind is free, even though Humankind's freedom is restricted. We are free within a situation, according to Frankl — that is, we are restricted by conditions. However, we are still free to choose our own stand toward the conditions. And we are free to choose to be a swine or to be a saint — to join the race of indecent human beings or the race of decent human beings.

As an example of Humankind's freedom, Frankl tells us about Dr. J. This man was known as "the mass murderer of Steinhof" because he was so diligent in sending psychotic individuals to their deaths during the Nazi reign. When the war ended, Dr. J was captured by the Soviets; however, one day the door to his cell stood open and so Frankl thought that he had escaped and gone to South America.

Many years later, Frankl discovered the truth. Dr. J had been taken to a Soviet prison camp, where he had died of cancer. However, a man who had been in prison with Dr. J testified of Dr. J's remarkable character. According to this man, Dr. J was the best friend it was possible to have and he had the highest possible moral character. So here is a man who changed himself from a swine into a saint. Therefore, Frankl asks, how can anyone doubt that Humankind "is ultimately self-determining"?

We are free.

Chapter 27: Dennis E. Bradford: The Meaning of Life

What is the meaning of life?

This is an important question because anyone reading this is alive, and so is faced with the question, What ought I to do? Also, all of us realize that death is not optional, and so it's important what we do with the limited time we spend in this life.

We can look at God in two ways: Either God exists, or God doesn't exist. If God doesn't exist, then we know that we and everything we have done or will do will vanish someday. One plausible scientific theory states that someday all the matter of the universe will be brought together by gravity and this time, instead of a Big Bang, we will have a Big Crunch.

Still, we can look at our lives as meaningful, Victor Frankl says. (Frankl is the author of *Man's Search for Meaning*, a memoir of the time he spent in a German concentration camp, and a description of the psychology of meaning that this experience led him to develop.) Instead of us regarding the days that we have lived as utterly vanished, we should instead regard them as having been "rescued from the past." None of us knows whether we will be alive tomorrow, but no one can change the past and what we have done in the past.

On the other hand, if we believe in God and an afterlife, we believe that God has put us on the Earth, and so we apparently need to do something here before we move on to the next life. It's unlikely that God simply wanted us to mark time during our existence on the Earth.

Each of us creates meaning through our Projects — that is, through what we choose to devote our time to doing in this life. All of us have many Projects. An important Project is simply acquiring the food, clothing, and shelter that are necessary for life. In addition, one person may have all of these Projects: being a student, a daughter, a wife, a mother, an artist, a part-time employee at the nearby day-care center, and many more.

Besides the Project of simply staying alive, an important Project for most of us will be our family relationships: raising a family and taking care of significant others and relatives. However, in addition to these very important Projects, we should choose — if possible — another Project to which we can devote our lives. I will call this a "central" Project.

In his book *A Thinker's Guide to Living Well* (published by Open Court), Dennis E. Bradford gives four suggestions for choosing a central Project:

1) The Project must be defensible.

Bradford states, "By 'defensible' I mean 'able to withstand rational scrutiny.' An indefensible Project is an indefensible life, a wasted life."

Not all Projects are defensible. Some people devote their lives to taking illegal drugs. Some people devote their lives to crime. Some people devote their lives to drinking alcohol.

According to Bradford, "The responsibility for what you do and for what you are is yours alone."

2) The good sought must be an end.

There is a difference between means and ends. You may want to become financially independent, and to do so you may have a job or your own business. In this example, your end or goal is to become financially independent, and your means to do so is your job or business. However, acquiring money should not be your central Project, because money is not an end in itself — we value money for what it can buy, not for what it is. After all, a USAmerican dollar is nothing more than a piece of paper (actually, cloth) printed with green ink.

According to Bradford, "The end of your Project should be something that is intrinsically valuable, good in itself, and not something that is only valuable as a means to something else."

3) The Project should be challenging, yet possible.

I would make a mistake if I were to have playing center for the Boston Celtics as the central Project of my life because I simply don't have the skills (or height) to achieve this Project. I need to make my central Project something that is achievable.

On the other hand, my central Project should be difficult. Many people devote their lives to becoming financially independent, but many people find this project not difficult enough. Many people are able to retire by age 50, and then they ask themselves, Now what do I do?

According to Bradford,

[...] the best kind of Project will involve as much creativity as possible. It is no good trying to be like everybody else, trying to avoid originality as if it were a disease. Try to be your own unique self: try to nurture whatever creative power you may have. Find a creative problem to just one of, or one part of, our many serious problems such as the risk of nuclear war, overpopulation, pollution, social injustice or misuse of natural resources and see how your own estimate of your own selfworth soars.

4) The Project should be a source of lasting satisfaction.
If your central Project fills you with stress, you have not chosen the right Project. According to Bradford, "Anyone who is engaged in an excellent Project will tend to obtain pleasure or satisfaction from it. Since the Project in question is the central one, it should be longlasting. If the activity is a continual source of lasting satisfaction, that pleasure is a sign that the activity is a good one."

At least three kinds of lives satisfy the four criteria above: a life of service and a life of inquiry and a life of creation. (Many other kinds of lives also satisfy the four criteria above.)

A life of service is devoted to helping other people. An example of a person devoting himself to a life of service is D. Cordell Brown, a Protestant minister who has cerebral palsy. After becoming a minister, he began to look for a way to serve other people, and he decided that services for handicapped adults were much needed. Therefore, he took his farm in Warsaw, Ohio, and turned it into Camp Echoing Hills, a camp for the handicapped. Next, he started a handicapped adult residence center at Echoing Hills, and he has started many other handicapped adult residences in Ohio, including Echoing Meadows in Athens, Ohio.

A life of inquiry is devoted to the acquisition of knowledge. In Athens, Ohio, there are numerous examples of lives of inquiry; all you have to do is to look at the professors of Ohio University. One example is retired philosophy professor Dr. Donald Borchert. He has several degrees, and he has written several books. In addition to devoting his life to inquiry, he has devoted his life to service, as is shown by the many philosophy courses he has taught.

A life of creation is devoted to artistic endeavors, such as the creation of art, music, and buildings (architecture). An example of a person who has devoted himself to a life of creation is Pablo Picasso, who was enormously prolific in creating art throughout his long life.

In her book *Girls to the Front: The True Story of the Riot GRRRL Revolution*, Sara Marcus wrote, "DIY [Do-It-Yourself] was a philosophy and a way of life, a touchstone that set its industrious adherents apart from the legions of USAmericans who passed their lives — as the punks saw it — trudging from TV set to first-run multiplex, from chain record store to commercial radio dial, treating art and culture as commodities to be consumed instead of vital forces to be struggled with and shaped, experimented with and created, breathed and lived."

Conclusion

The choice of your central Project belongs to you only. Only you can decide what to do with your life.

Addendum to college students: Deciding on your central Project can be a big help in choosing a major. Decide what your central Project will be, then choose a major that will help you achieve your central Project.

Chapter 28: Socrates (circa 470 B.C.E.-399 B.C.E.): Philosophy

The ancient Greek philosopher Socrates (circa 470 B.C.E.-399 B.C.E.) was a model philosopher and so reading Plato's *Apology* is a good place to start a study of philosophy. It is also a good place to see how Socrates found meaning in his life.

First, a little background information. Despite the name of *Apology* for this dialogue by Plato, Socrates did not apologize for anything. Instead, he offered a spirited defense in the Athenian law courts after being accused of corrupting the youth of Athens and not believing in the gods that everyone else believed in. (The Greek word used for the title of Plato's dialogue means "defense," not "apology.")

In addition to being a model philosopher, Socrates was a model teacher. He never took money for teaching, but among his pupils was Plato, who later became the teacher of Aristotle, who later became the teacher of Alexander the Great of Macedon.

Readers should be aware that Socrates did not write down any of his ideas. However, in most of the dialogues written by Plato, Socrates is the main speaker. Scholars disagree over how much of what the character "Socrates" says in Plato's dialogues can actually be attributed to the real, historical Socrates; however, scholars believe that the earlier dialogues state the historical Socrates' ideas. In the later dialogues, Plato built on the philosophical foundation of Socrates' ideas.

The *Apology* is probably an early dialogue. Readers should note that Plato attended Socrates' trial.

The Wisdom of Socrates

To begin his defense, Socrates told the story of how he acquired his reputation for wisdom. Apparently Socrates was always a debater, for his friend Chaerephon went to Delphi to ask the priestess there whether Socrates was the wisest man on earth.

(The Delphic Oracle was dedicated to the Greek god Apollo and the priestesses there had the reputation of being able to foretell the future. Note: An oracle is a prophet or a priestess — someone who foretells the future.

Unfortunately, the priestesses acquired this reputation by being vague in their replies. When the king of Lydia, Croesus, asked the oracle whether he should attack Persia, she replied, "If you attack Persia, a mighty kingdom will fall." Croesus did attack Persia, but the mighty kingdom that fell was his own.)

The priestess replied to Chaerephon (in non-vague language) that Socrates was the wisest man on earth, thus shocking Socrates, who felt that he knew very little. To prove the priestess false, Socrates began questioning people, especially people who had a reputation for being wise. Unfortunately, Socrates discovered that these people did not deserve their reputation for wisdom. Although they often knew things that Socrates did not, they made the mistake of thinking that they knew things that they did not know. This is a mistake that Socrates did not make; when he didn't know something, he was aware of his ignorance. To show people that often they didn't know something although they thought they did, Socrates used the philosophical technique known as indirect proof.

Indirect Proof

Basically, the method of indirect proof works like this: First, you start with an assumption. Then, through a series of logical steps you show that the assumption leads to a contradiction. If an assumption logically leads to a contradiction, we know that the assumption must be incorrect and therefore we are justified in rejecting it.

In Plato's dialogue *Euthyphro*, we can see Socrates in action using indirect proof to show that Euthyphro, a reciter of poetry, has opinions that are incorrect. Socrates asked Euthyphro for a definition of piety, and after some wrangling, got this definition out of him: What is pious is pleasing to the gods, and what is impious is not pleasing to the gods. (To understand this example, readers must remember that the ancients believed in many gods, unlike today's Jews and Christians.)

Socrates then showed that this assumption logically leads to a contradiction by pointing out that what pleases some gods will not please other gods. For example, if you remember *The Iliad* by Homer, you know that the Trojan War was fought between two groups of people: the Greeks and the Trojans. Some of the gods favored the Greeks, while other gods favored the Trojans. Aphrodite, the goddess of love, favored the Trojans while Athena, the goddess of wisdom, favored the Greeks. Therefore, a battle in which the Trojans defeated the Greeks would please Aphrodite but not Athena.

As you can see, Euthyphro's definition (his assumption) leads to a contradiction: the same action (the battle) is, at the same time, both pious (because pleasing to Aphrodite) and impious (because not pleasing to Athena). One fact of logic and of mathematics that cannot be disputed is that something cannot be what it is and, at the same time, not what it is. It is impossible for a triangle to be both a triangle and a square at the same time. It is impossible for a positive integer to be both a positive integer and a negative integer at the same time.

Socrates as a Critical and as a Constructive Philosopher

Obviously, Socrates was a keen critic of others' ideas, as we saw above in his criticism of Euthyphro's definition of "piety." An important function of philosophy is to show us when our ideas are contradictory or otherwise confused. However, Socrates was also a constructive philosopher. He performed a valuable function by showing people when their ideas were confused. After all, you are not likely to seek knowledge of something you think you already know. Only after you discover that you don't know something will you take steps to remedy the deficiency in your thinking.

After all, when Euthyphro thinks that he knows what piety is, he doesn't consider searching for knowledge about piety. Why try to learn something that you already think you know? However, once Socrates shows that Euthyphro is mistaken in his definition of piety, then Euthyphro may become willing to begin the search for knowledge about piety.

Why People Disliked Socrates

People disliked Socrates for at least two reasons. First, Socrates was like a stinging fly to the important people of Athens. In his dialogues with these VIPs, Socrates consistently showed that these people thought that they knew something when they did not really know much — if anything — about it. Even when Socrates found someone who knew something that Socrates did not know, such as a potter, the person who knew something in one area thought that he knew something in an area where he had no knowledge at all. Socrates had the advantage over these people because at least he knew when he had no knowledge — Socrates was aware of his ignorance.

The second major reason that people disliked Socrates was because young people imitated him. Young people followed Socrates and learned his techniques of debate through watching him debate other people. The young people would imitate Socrates by engaging VIPs in debate and showing — in front of other people in public places — that the VIPs were ignorant.

It's no wonder that Socrates was so hated because both he and his followers used indirect proof to show that many people who were reputed as being wise were actually ignorant. At the trial, the accusers represented different groups of people who were angry at Socrates. Meletus, a poet, was angry at Socrates. Anytus, a professional man and politician, was angry at Socrates. Lycaon, an orator, was angry at Socrates. All three accusers wanted Socrates to be condemned to death.

Socrates as a Defender of Free Speech

Greek trials had two parts. In the first part of the trial, the prosecutors and the accused presented their cases and then the jury voted the defendant either guilty or not guilty. If the defendant was found guilty, then the trial moved on to the second part, in which both the prosecutors and the accused proposed different punishments. Of course, the prosecutors would ask for a harsh penalty, and the accused would ask for a lighter penalty. The jury would then vote on which penalty would be given to the accused (who, of course, has already been found guilty).

Before the vote to determine his guilt was taken, although Socrates knew that he could probably get off by promising to stop engaging people in philosophical dialogue, he declined to restrict his free speech; instead, he told the jury that he would continue to do philosophy just as he had done before the trial.

Socrates was found guilty, so the jury then listened to different penalties that could be assessed against Socrates. The accusers asked for the death penalty. Scholars believe that if Socrates had proposed exile as a penalty, the jury probably would have accepted this penalty. However, Socrates rejected exile: He said that if he left Athens and went to another city-state to live, he would continue to do philosophy and thus run into the same trouble as before. According to Socrates, "The unexamined life is not worth living." The examined life is the life of philosophy, of inquiring into the truth about important issues.

Socrates then spoke about how valuable he was to Athens. By engaging the citizens of Athens in dialogue and by showing them where their ideas are confused, Socrates involved the citizens of Athens in philosophy. Of course, some of the citizens did not like this process — at the end of the *Euthyphro*, Euthyphro couldn't wait to get away from Socrates! However, Socrates compared himself to a stinging fly that won't let the citizens rest.

Because Socrates regarded himself as so valuable to Athens, after he had been found guilty and was asked to propose a punishment for himself, Socrates proposed that he be given free room and board at the public expense! However, some of his friends at the trial, including Plato, asked that he instead propose a fine of money, which they would pay for him.

Death

Because he declined to stop philosophizing, Socrates' proposal of a fine of money was rejected and instead he was condemned to death. A month later Socrates was executed; he was given poison hemlock to drink. However, Socrates' death was not for nothing — he died as both a martyr to philosophy and to free speech. (Without free speech, philosophy cannot flourish.)

Interestingly, Socrates was not afraid of death. He said at the end of the *Apology* that death is one of two things, neither of which is to be feared:

1) Death is like a long dreamless sleep. In this case, death is the extinguishing of consciousness. We will not feel pain or anything else, so we ought not to fear this kind of death.

2) Death is like a journey to another place where we shall live again. There Socrates will meet the heroes of ancient Greece and engage in philosophical debate. This, Socrates says, would be very good indeed.

Other dialogues of Plato, such as the *Phaedo*, make clear that Socrates believed in immortality. I encourage students to read the last scene of the *Phaedo*, which recounts the death of Socrates.

Plato's *Apology* is one of the great books of Western civilization; it should be re-read annually.

Note: Plato's *Apology* has been translated many, many times.

APPENDIX A: FAIR USE

This book uses many short quotations from various works. This use is consistent with fair use:

§ 107. Limitations on exclusive rights: Fair use Release date: 2004-04-30

Notwithstanding the provisions of sections 106 and 106A, the fair use of a copyrighted work, including such use by reproduction in copies or phonorecords or by any other means specified by that section, for purposes such as criticism, comment, news reporting, teaching (including multiple copies for classroom use), scholarship, or research, is not an infringement of copyright. In determining whether the use made of a work in any particular case is a fair use the factors to be considered shall include —

(1) the purpose and character of the use, including whether such use is of a commercial nature or is for nonprofit educational purposes;

(2) the nature of the copyrighted work;

(3) the amount and substantiality of the portion used in relation to the copyrighted work as a whole; and

(4) the effect of the use upon the potential market for or value of the copyrighted work.

The fact that a work is unpublished shall not itself bar a finding of fair use if such finding is made upon consideration of all the above factors.

Source of Fair Use information: <http://www.law.cornell.edu/uscode/text/17/107>.

APPENDIX B: ABOUT THE AUTHOR

It was a dark and stormy night. Suddenly a cry rang out, and on a hot summer night in 1954, Josephine, wife of Carl Bruce, gave birth to a boy — me. Unfortunately, this young married couple allowed Reuben Saturday, Josephine's brother, to name their first-born. Reuben, aka "The Joker," decided that Bruce was a nice name, so he decided to name me Bruce Bruce. I have gone by my middle name — David — ever since.

Being named Bruce David Bruce hasn't been all bad. Bank tellers remember me very quickly, so I don't often have to show an ID. It can be fun in charades, also. When I was a counselor as a teenager at Camp Echoing Hills in Warsaw, Ohio, a fellow counselor gave the signs for "sounds like" and "two words," then she pointed to a bruise on her leg twice. Bruise Bruise? Oh yeah, Bruce Bruce is the answer!

Uncle Reuben, by the way, gave me a haircut when I was in kindergarten. He cut my hair short and shaved a small bald spot on the back of my head. My mother wouldn't let me go to school until the bald spot grew out again.

Of all my brothers and sisters (six in all), I am the only transplant to Athens, Ohio. I was born in Newark, Ohio, and have lived all around Southeastern Ohio. However, I moved to Athens to go to Ohio University and have never left.

At Ohio U, I never could make up my mind whether to major in English or Philosophy, so I got a bachelor's degree with a double major in both areas, then I added a master's degree in English and a master's degree in Philosophy. Currently, and for a long time to come, I publish a weekly humorous column titled "Wise Up!" for *The Athens News* and I am a retired English instructor at Ohio U.

If all goes well, I will publish one or two books a year for the rest of my life. (On the other hand, a good way to make God laugh is to tell Her your plans.)

By the way, my sister Brenda Kennedy writes romances such as *A New Beginning* and *Shattered Dreams*.

APPENDIX C: SOME BOOKS BY DAVID BRUCE

Philosophy for the Masses Series

Philosophy for the Masses: Ethics

Philosophy for the Masses: Metaphysics and More

Philosophy for the Masses: Religion

Retellings of a Classic Work of Literature

Arden of Faversham: *A Retelling*

Ben Jonson's The Alchemist: *A Retelling*

Ben Jonson's The Arraignment, or Poetaster: *A Retelling*

Ben Jonson's Bartholomew Fair: *A Retelling*

Ben Jonson's The Case is Altered: *A Retelling*

Ben Jonson's Catiline's Conspiracy: *A Retelling*

Ben Jonson's The Devil is an Ass: *A Retelling*

Ben Jonson's Epicene: *A Retelling*

Ben Jonson's Every Man in His Humor: *A Retelling*

Ben Jonson's Every Man Out of His Humor: *A Retelling*

Ben Jonson's The Fountain of Self-Love, or Cynthia's Revels: *A Retelling*

Ben Jonson's The Magnetic Lady, or Humors Reconciled: *A Retelling*

Ben Jonson's The New Inn, or The Light Heart: *A Retelling*

Ben Jonson's Sejanus' Fall: *A Retelling*

Ben Jonson's The Staple of News: *A Retelling*

Ben Jonson's A Tale of a Tub: *A Retelling*

Ben Jonson's Volpone, or the Fox: *A Retelling*

Christopher Marlowe's Complete Plays: Retellings

Christopher Marlowe's Dido, Queen of Carthage: *A Retelling*

Christopher Marlowe's Doctor Faustus: *Retellings of the 1604 A-Text and of the 1616 B-Text*

Christopher Marlowe's Edward II: *A Retelling*

Christopher Marlowe's The Massacre at Paris: *A Retelling*

Christopher Marlowe's The Rich Jew of Malta: *A Retelling*

Christopher Marlowe's Tamburlaine, Parts 1 and 2: *Retellings*

Dante's Divine Comedy: *A Retelling in Prose*

Dante's Inferno: *A Retelling in Prose*

Dante's Purgatory: *A Retelling in Prose*

Dante's Paradise: *A Retelling in Prose*

The Famous Victories of Henry V: *A Retelling*

From the Iliad *to the* Odyssey: *A Retelling in Prose of Quintus of Smyrna's* Posthomerica

George Chapman, Ben Jonson, and John Marston's Eastward Ho! *A Retelling*

George Peele's The Arraignment of Paris: *A Retelling*

William Shakespeare's 5 Late Romances: Retellings in Prose
William Shakespeare's 10 Histories: Retellings in Prose
William Shakespeare's 11 Tragedies: Retellings in Prose
William Shakespeare's 12 Comedies: Retellings in Prose
William Shakespeare's 38 Plays: Retellings in Prose
William Shakespeare's 1 Henry IV, aka Henry IV, Part 1: A Retelling in Prose
William Shakespeare's 2 Henry IV, aka Henry IV, Part 2: A Retelling in Prose
William Shakespeare's 1 Henry VI, aka Henry VI, Part 1: A Retelling in Prose
William Shakespeare's 2 Henry VI, aka Henry VI, Part 2: A Retelling in Prose
William Shakespeare's 3 Henry VI, aka Henry VI, Part 3: A Retelling in Prose
William Shakespeare's All's Well that Ends Well: A Retelling in Prose
William Shakespeare's Antony and Cleopatra: A Retelling in Prose
William Shakespeare's As You Like It: A Retelling in Prose
William Shakespeare's The Comedy of Errors: A Retelling in Prose
William Shakespeare's Coriolanus: A Retelling in Prose
William Shakespeare's Cymbeline: A Retelling in Prose
William Shakespeare's Hamlet: A Retelling in Prose
William Shakespeare's Henry V: A Retelling in Prose
William Shakespeare's Henry VIII: A Retelling in Prose
William Shakespeare's Julius Caesar: A Retelling in Prose
William Shakespeare's King John: A Retelling in Prose
William Shakespeare's King Lear: A Retelling in Prose
William Shakespeare's Love's Labor's Lost: A Retelling in Prose
William Shakespeare's Macbeth: A Retelling in Prose
William Shakespeare's Measure for Measure: A Retelling in Prose
William Shakespeare's The Merchant of Venice: A Retelling in Prose
William Shakespeare's The Merry Wives of Windsor: A Retelling in Prose
William Shakespeare's A Midsummer Night's Dream: A Retelling in Prose
William Shakespeare's Much Ado About Nothing: A Retelling in Prose
William Shakespeare's Othello: A Retelling in Prose
William Shakespeare's Pericles, Prince of Tyre: A Retelling in Prose
William Shakespeare's Richard II: A Retelling in Prose
William Shakespeare's Richard III: A Retelling in Prose
William Shakespeare's Romeo and Juliet: A Retelling in Prose
William Shakespeare's The Taming of the Shrew: A Retelling in Prose
William Shakespeare's The Tempest: A Retelling in Prose
William Shakespeare's Timon of Athens: A Retelling in Prose
William Shakespeare's Titus Andronicus: A Retelling in Prose
William Shakespeare's Troilus and Cressida: A Retelling in Prose
William Shakespeare's Twelfth Night: A Retelling in Prose
William Shakespeare's The Two Gentlemen of Verona: A Retelling in Prose
William Shakespeare's The Two Noble Kinsmen: A Retelling in Prose

William Shakespeare's The Winter's Tale: *A Retelling in Prose*
Anecdote Books
250 Anecdotes About Opera
250 Anecdotes About Religion
250 Anecdotes About Religion: Volume 2
The Coolest People in Art: 250 Anecdotes
The Coolest People in Books: 250 Anecdotes
The Coolest People in Comedy: 250 Anecdotes
Don't Fear the Reaper: 250 Anecdotes
The Funniest People in Art: 250 Anecdotes
The Funniest People in Books: 250 Anecdotes
The Funniest People in Books, Volume 2: 250 Anecdotes
The Funniest People in Books, Volume 3: 250 Anecdotes
The Funniest People in Comedy: 250 Anecdotes
The Funniest People in Dance: 250 Anecdotes
The Funniest People in Families: 250 Anecdotes
The Funniest People in Families, Volume 2: 250 Anecdotes
The Funniest People in Families, Volume 3: 250 Anecdotes
The Funniest People in Families, Volume 4: 250 Anecdotes
The Funniest People in Families, Volume 5: 250 Anecdotes
The Funniest People in Families, Volume 6: 250 Anecdotes
The Funniest People in Movies: 250 Anecdotes
The Funniest People in Music: 250 Anecdotes
The Funniest People in Music, Volume 2: 250 Anecdotes
The Funniest People in Music, Volume 3: 250 Anecdotes
The Funniest People in Neighborhoods: 250 Anecdotes
The Funniest People in Relationships: 250 Anecdotes
The Funniest People in Sports: 250 Anecdotes
The Funniest People in Sports, Volume 2: 250 Anecdotes
The Funniest People in Television and Radio: 250 Anecdotes
The Funniest People in Theater: 250 Anecdotes
The Funniest People Who Live Life: 250 Anecdotes
The Funniest People Who Live Life, Volume 2: 250 Anecdotes
The Kindest People Who Do Good Deeds, Volume 1: 250 Anecdotes
The Kindest People Who Do Good Deeds, Volume 2: 250 Anecdotes
Maximum Cool: 250 Anecdotes
The Most Interesting People in Movies: 250 Anecdotes
The Most Interesting People in Politics and History: 250 Anecdotes
The Most Interesting People in Politics and History, Volume 2: 250 Anecdotes
The Most Interesting People in Politics and History, Volume 3: 250 Anecdotes
The Most Interesting People in Religion: 250 Anecdotes
The Most Interesting People in Sports: 250 Anecdotes

The Most Interesting People Who Live Life: 250 Anecdotes
The Most Interesting People Who Live Life, Volume 2: 250 Anecdotes
Resist Psychic Death: 250 Anecdotes
Seize the Day: 250 Anecdotes and Stories
Children's Biography
Nadia Comaneci: Perfect Ten

APPENDIX D: SOME BOOKS BY BRENDA KENNEDY (MY SISTER)

The Forgotten Trilogy
  Book One: *Forgetting the Past*
  Book Two: *Living for Today*
  Book Three: *Seeking the Future*
The Learning to Live Trilogy
  Book One: *Learning to Live*
  Book Two: *Learning to Trust*
  Book Three: *Learning to Love*
The Starting Over Trilogy
  Book One: *A New Beginning*
  Book Two: *Saving Angel*
  Book Three: *Destined to Love*
The Freedom Trilogy
  Book One: *Shattered Dreams*
  Book Two: *Broken Lives*
  Book Three: *Mending Hearts*
The Fighting to Survive Trilogy
  Round One: *A Life Worth Fighting*
  Round Two: *Against the Odds*
  Round Three: *One Last Fight*
The Rose Farm Trilogy
  Book One: *Forever Country*
  Book Two: *Country Life*
  Book Three: *Country Love*
Books in the Seashell Island Stand-alone Series
  Book One: *Home on Seashell Island* (Free)
  Book Two: *Christmas on Seashell Island*
  Book Three: *Living on Seashell Island*
  Book Four: *Moving to Seashell Island*
  Book Five: *Returning to Seashell Island*
Books in the Pineapple Grove Cozy Murder Mystery Stand-alone Series
  Book One: *Murder Behind the Coffeehouse*
  Book Two: *Murder in the Library*
Books in the Montgomery Wine Stand-alone Series
  Book One: *A Place to Call Home*
  Book Two: *In Search of Happiness...* coming soon

Stand-alone books in the "Another Round of Laughter Series" written by Brenda and some of her siblings: Carla Evans, Martha Farmer, Rosa Jones, and David Bruce.

Cupcakes Are Not a Diet Food (Free)

Kids Are Not Always Angels

Aging Is Not for Sissies

www.ingramcontent.com/pod-product-compliance
Lightning Source LLC
Chambersburg PA
CBHW031412150726
47989CB00002B/625